[*Enter Jesus*]

49 DAYS
FINDING PEACE, HOPE, JOY, &
TRUTH IN THE SAVIOR

Gwendolen Henry

WESTBOW
PRESS®
A DIVISION OF THOMAS NELSON
& ZONDERVAN

WestBow Press books may be ordered through booksellers or by contacting:

WestBow Press
A Division of Thomas Nelson & Zondervan
1663 Liberty Drive
Bloomington, IN 47403
www.westbowpress.com
844-714-3454

Scripture marked (NKJV) taken from the New King James Version®. Copyright © 1982 by Thomas Nelson. Used by permission. All rights reserved.

Scripture quotations marked (GNT) are from the Good News Translation in Today's English Version- Second Edition Copyright © 1992 by American Bible Society. Used by Permission.

Scripture marked (KJV) taken from the King James Version of the Bible.

ISBN: 978-1-6642-7764-9 (sc)
ISBN: 978-1-6642-7763-2 (hc)
ISBN: 978-1-6642-7765-6 (e)

Library of Congress Control Number: 2022916647

Print information available on the last page.

WestBow Press rev. date: 10/18/2022

CONTENTS

DEDICATION

This devotional is dedicated to my family: to my daughter and son, who gave me the most important job in the world; my husband, my true love and helpmate; my grandchildren, for keeping me young and filling my heart with more joy than I thought possible; my mom, a godly example of serving others; my brother and friend, of whom I am so proud; my mother-in-law, who has always treated me with kindness; and my friends and former work family, whom I value, cherish, and respect more than words can express. Most of all, I dedicate this book to Jesus, my Savior, who no longer has a supporting role but is front and center in my life story.

INTRODUCTION

On April 25, 2019, I was confronted with a bizarre "did you know?" statement regarding the apostle Paul. Although it's practically unheard of, I was rendered speechless. Certain the information was false but unable to provide a fact-based comeback, I prayed for the Lord's guidance. After a sincere plea for Him to reveal who Paul *really* was, the answer was literally provided to me in black and white. The following day, I picked up my Bible, which was still open from the night before. It was not, however, open to where I'd left it. My eyes fell to the lower right-hand portion of scripture, and there was the answer to my question, in dramatic *here it is* fashion. My prayer wasn't answered by a thundering voice from above, but it *was* answered—through God's existing word. This set me on a path to discover who God, Jesus and the Holy Spirit are. Not who I thought they were, but the God, Jesus, and Holy Spirit of the Bible.

When deciding upon a title for this devotional, I imagined writing a movie script—a chaotic, action drama. With each character's life in turmoil, the movie would need a powerful, commanding protagonist to sweep in and save the day. While researching stage directions and drama phrases, I was drawn to the term *Enter,* a stage direction indicating the introduction of a character onto the scene. So here we are, struggling in a hectic world, feeling exhausted and alone, at our wits end, nowhere to turn, thinking all is lost, when suddenly—[Enter Jesus].

Each one of these forty-nine devotions is personal. You could say I wrote them for myself as I studied specific topics. Although we each have unique stories, we share similar experiences of fear, doubt, anxiety, and hopelessness. God never intended for us to face these challenges alone. He wants to be our "refuge and strength, a very present help in trouble" (Psalm 46:1). He doesn't want us to call upon Him only in times of despair. He wants a daily relationship with us. Jesus wants to be front and center, the main character in our lives, and to develop a personal connection with us that will deepen over time.

I'm so thankful the plea of this profoundly flawed, overreacting micromanager was heard. Since that day, the Holy Spirit has been softening specific areas of my life that were once hardened, and things that used to anger me now cause genuine sorrow. But, unfortunately, this means I cry a lot more.

I sincerely pray that everyone who reads this devotional is blessed, strengthens their faith—and maybe laughs just a little.

All biblical citations are from the New King James Version unless otherwise noted.

He has no form or comeliness; and when we see Him,
there is no beauty that we should desire Him.
(Isaiah 53:2)

NO BEAUTY

I'm going to be honest—I prayed for beautiful children. Stay with me, and don't judge just yet. I was a late bloomer and an unattractive child. Lest anyone think I exaggerate, my fourth-grade yearbook photo had me styling a pair of silver stop-sign glasses, jagged bangs, and an uneven mullet-style haircut that would bring tears to the eyes of Billy Ray Cyrus. When I found out I was pregnant with a little girl my prayer for beauty was reflexive. I couldn't bear the thought of someone making fun of her the way others made fun of me. So retrieving this memory of my teenage daughter from one of those tightly sealed compartments of whatever makes up my brain is painful.

She was thirteen years old and sobbing. This time the tears were because her naturally curly hair, which nobody else had, wasn't pretty *enough*. As she cried, I thought, *How is it possible for anyone to make this child feel not beautiful?* She is quite literally beautiful, inside and out, with a heart as big as the world. And though God had answered my prayer, beauty is in the eye of the beholder. And on that particular day the beholder was a thirteen-year-old boy.

I may not have said it then, I don't remember, but I'd said it before. As a parent, you've probably said it—or perhaps it was said to you: it's what's on the inside that counts. When we tell our children, or anyone else, that loyalty, character, and kindness are more important qualities than physical beauty or popularity, why should they believe us? In *their* mind, in *their* world, at *that* moment, all they know is they are being made to feel *less than*.

Once I became a mother, finally having realized my worth was found in the One who created me, teaching and exemplifying kindness to others was a parenting priority. The lemons I had no control over as a child were used to make lemonade; God took something bitter and turned it into something sweet and purposeful, albeit twenty years later. Although I eventually came out stronger on the other side, tragically, far too many children and young adults do not. Bullying has metastasized from school hallways and locker rooms to social media. Cowards armed with a keyboard viciously inflict harm, which I, as a young mother, could not have imagined in my worst nightmares.

[Enter Jesus]

In the focus verse, the prophet Isaiah foretold the coming of the Messiah and wrote that He would have *no beauty*. For just a moment, think about those two words and what they really mean—Jesus was plain and there was absolutely nothing physically compelling about Him. So what was the deal? How did this unassuming man convince twelve others to turn their lives upside down and follow Him? What made thousands of people drop what they were doing and sit on a hillside to hear Him speak? How did He gather a following *so* large that it threatened the religious rulers of the day? The answer, like Jesus' earthly appearance, is plain. People were drawn to Him because of what was on the *inside*. He was God, in the form of an average-looking man. It was His calming presence, compassion, confidence, and supernatural authority that captivated them.

So, if someone you love is being made to feel *less than,* tell them about ordinary-looking Jesus. Tell them to turn to the One who said, "Before I formed you in the womb I knew you" (Jeremiah 1:5), and you are "fearfully and wonderfully made" (Psalm 139:14). Our heavenly Father created us *exactly* the way He wanted—for *His* purpose.

I recently told my grandson that Jesus had *no beauty*—because in a world obsessed with outward appearances, it's never too early to begin teaching children about what truly matters. I told him this man, with no outward appeal, turned out to be the most influential and important man in the history of the world—because of what was on the *inside*.

Thoughts and Reflection

What are some ways you can instill humble confidence in your children or grandchildren? How can you encourage your child or grandchild to be kind and stand up for those who are unable to stand up for themselves?

Prayer

Dear Heavenly Father, help me to pray so effectively for my children and grandchildren that Satan trembles at my fervent prayers in Your holy name. Help me, and them, find our identities in You, and You alone.

Then the scribes and Pharisees brought to Him a woman
caught in adultery. And when they had set her in the midst,
they said to Him, "Teacher, this woman was caught in
adultery, in the very act. Now Moses, in the law, commanded
us that such should be stoned. But what do You say?"
(John 8:3–5)

STONES, ROCKS, AND HARD PLACES

*I*magine it's the first century. You're in your own home, when suddenly a mob of self-righteous, angry men storm inside. You know why they've come. They grab you, drag you through the streets, and throw you at the feet of a controversial new Teacher. You know you're guilty—by law. Surrounded by pious religious leaders glaring down in disgust, you lower your gaze to the ground. Ashamed and terrified, you hear one of them say three words that will sentence you to death: "caught in adultery." Your body shakes and you begin to sob uncontrollably. Then one among the mob asks of the Teacher, "But what do You say?" And now you wait.

[Enter Jesus]

Jesus was in the temple preaching when the scribes and Pharisees brought the woman to Him. The accusation wasn't hearsay; she was caught in the very act, and per the Mosaic Law she should be put to death (Leviticus 20:10–12). The Pharisees brought the woman to Jesus and asked His opinion so "that they might have something of which to accuse Him" (John 8:6). Jesus taught love, mercy, and forgiveness. If He agreed to stone her, He would violate His own teachings. If He spared her life, He would be violating the Mosaic Law. They were literally attempting to wedge Jesus between a rock and a hard place.

With great wisdom, Jesus didn't say a word. He instead "stooped down and wrote on the ground with His finger, as though He did not hear" (John 8:6). I imagine this infuriated the Pharisees. They thought they finally had Him, but He ignored their question. So, what did Jesus write in the dirt? A few months ago, I watched a movie, *The Resurrection of Gavin Stone*, written by Andrea Gyerston Nasfell and directed by Dallas Jenkins. The actor portraying Jesus in this temple scene knelt and wrote the word "grace" in the sand. It was a beautiful illustration of God's mercy, but is that actually what Jesus wrote?

Although we won't know the true answer until we are face-to-face with Him, I believe Jesus wrote something else. The Bible records two other specific instances when words were written by the hand of God. In Daniel 5:24–28, Daniel records the "fingers of the hand" writing on the wall of the palace, communicating to Belshazzar that his kingdom was finished, and he had been "weighed in the balances and found wanting." The book of Exodus recounts the Israelites being freed from slavery in Egypt and crossing the desert to Mount Sinai. Moses scaled the mountain, and "when He [God] had made an end of speaking with him on Mount Sinai, He gave Moses two tablets of the Testimony, tablets of stone, written with the finger of God" (Exodus 31:18). Since the Pharisees brought up the Mosaic Law, I believe what Jesus wrote in the dirt was related to the Ten Commandments.

After His initial writing, Jesus stood and said, "He who is without sin among you, let him throw a stone at her first" (John 8:7). He knelt down *again* and continued. So, whatever He was writing took some time. I believe what Jesus scrawled in the dirt was the Ten Commandments, by which we will all be judged. When He challenged the angry mob with the *"He who is without sin"* statement, "those who heard it, being convicted by their conscience, went out one by one, beginning with the oldest even to the last" (John 8:9). Jesus was now alone with the woman. He stood up and saw that those who had condemned her were gone, and then said to her, "'Woman, where are those accusers of yours? Has no one condemned you?' She said, 'No one, Lord.' And Jesus said to her, 'Neither do I condemn you; go and sin no more'" (John 8:10–11).

Thoughts and Reflection

The same loving compassion Jesus extended to the woman caught in adultery can be yours. His same mercy can be yours: "If we confess our sins, He is faithful and just to forgive us our sins and to cleanse us from all unrighteousness" (1 John 1:9).

Prayer

Dear heavenly Father, thank You for Your forgiveness and mercy. Help me to show the same compassion to others that You have shown to me.

These things I have spoken to you, that in Me you may
have peace. In the world you will have tribulation; but
be of good cheer, I have overcome the world.
(John 16:33)

SUPERNATURAL PEACE

In 2015, a video was released by Libyan militants loyal to ISIS showing the beheading of twenty-one Egyptian Christians. They calmly walked along the beach and knelt in front of the camera as ISIS soldiers, masked in black, stood behind them with sheathed swords. Their composure was surreal. Despite being in the presence of palpable evil and realizing what was about to happen, there was no panic, no crying, no begging for mercy, and no apparent fear. There was peace—supernatural peace. As they knelt onto the sand, I couldn't help but wonder what was racing through their minds. Did their life flash before them? Were they thinking of their families? Were they silently praying? Were they meditating on a particular passage in the Bible? One verse that stands out among all others for such a time as this is: "Be strong and of good courage, do not fear, nor be afraid of them; for the Lord your God, He is the One who goes with you. He will not leave you nor forsake you" (Deuteronomy 31:6).

In twenty-first century America we don't experience persecution like Christians in other parts of the world, yet we experience fear on a daily basis. As individuals we may receive a life-altering medical diagnosis. As parents, we fear the indoctrination our children and grandchildren are receiving in the public education system. We fear for their safety in schools, where there is now a need to practice active shooter drills. Media outlets constantly bombard us with doom and gloom scenarios and fill us with overwhelming anxiety about the world in general. During a tear-filled (on my end) conversation with my husband regarding a situation with our children he said, "I see where you're coming from. It's human nature to worry and want to fix things. It's *not* human nature to hand our worries over to God. But you have access to this power, power to hand them completely over. Why aren't you doing it?"

[Enter Jesus]

My husband's loving, but firm, message was clear—get a grip. More importantly, Jesus' message is clear: we *will* have tribulation in this life, but we can *also* have peace; supernatural peace. Turning loved ones over to God and trusting Him to guide and shield them is challenging to say the least. My mom once said, "We put something in God's hands today, but take it back tomorrow"—because *we* want control. Surrendering fear and worry is intentional; we must *decide* to do it. That my yielding was neither natural nor easy for me is an epic understatement. Admittedly, I like control, and I want to fix everything and everyone. Nevertheless, once I got it through my head that God is the great *I Am,* and this writer is the great *I'm not,* I began letting go of the uncontrollable.

Don't misunderstand; I'm all about being prepared for life's uncertainties. September 11 taught me that. Having extra food and medical supplies on hand, teaching children what to do when they're lost, and having them memorize phone numbers are wise precautions. Preparedness prevents panic and lessens fear in many situations. However, no amount of fear, worry, or preparedness will protect our loved ones 100 percent of the time.

We are all weak of flesh and a work in progress. But God tells us: "He gives power to the weak, and to those who have no might He increases strength" (Isaiah 40:29). There are times when I still worry, and jokingly say that I need twelve hours after being blindsided by the unexpected before I can release it to God. It used to be forty-eight, so there's progress. We're human and God knows our fears and weaknesses. But so does Satan. The evil one can steal our joy and rob us of God's intended peace, and he's masterful at it. However, Jesus told us He has overcome the world. Now all we have to do is believe it and place our *tiny* amount of faith into the hands of a *big* God.

Thoughts and Reflection

What are some of your greatest fears? How does Satan use them against you? How can you more effectively release fear to the One who repeatedly tells us to "fear not"?

Prayer

Dear heavenly Father, I cannot do this on my own. At times fear cripples me. Help me to trust in You. Please reveal *Your* strength through *my* weakness and replace my fear with Your supernatural peace.

*And I looked, and behold, in the midst of the throne
and of the four living creatures, and in the midst of the
elders, stood a Lamb as though it had been slain.
(Revelation 5:6)*

THE BIG PICTURE

*M*y husband and I recently joined a life group at our church, the purpose of which is to develop friendships and discuss the previous Sunday sermon. One evening, our group leader read from Revelation 5. His voice cracked as he read. When he finished, he looked up, his wife handed him a tissue, and he asked the group, "Didn't you think that was beautiful?" There was silence. I glanced at my husband, who, as usual, had no visible sign of what he was thinking on his face. Finally, another lady in our group said, "No. I didn't find it beautiful." The flood gates were now open, and I chimed in, "That's a no for me, too. It was horrible and it makes me angry—nothing beautiful about it." All I could visualize was Jesus as the *slain lamb,* turned over to Pilate by the Jewish leaders and beaten and bloodied by the Romans. I was hyper focused on those two words and ignored the rest of the chapter. I had tunnel vision and couldn't see the forest for the trees. Or rather, I couldn't see the beauty for the blood. The study continued, and over the following days I pondered the rest of the chapter.

[Enter Jesus]

The disciple John had been exiled to the island of Patmos and was given a vision. He recorded the vision in the book of Revelation. John writes, "You are worthy to take the scroll, and to open its seals; for You were slain, and have redeemed us to God by Your blood out of every tribe and tongue and people and nation, and have made us kings and priests to our God; and we shall reign on the earth …

Blessing and honor and glory and power be to Him who sits on the throne, and to the Lamb, forever and ever" (Revelation 5:9–13). Of note, this passage was also read during our life group—I just didn't hear it. After rereading the chapter later in the week, however, I thought, *That really is beautiful and full of hope.* No longer nailed to a cross, struggling to breathe, scourged and unrecognizable, Jesus is now at the right hand of God, receiving the worship He deserves. Revelation, for all its imagery and symbolism, reveals the worthiness of Jesus and the hope we have in Him. His holiness is, and for eternity will be, the subject of angelic song and saintly praise.

In today's society, not many people see Jesus as the big picture. We're too busy with our own lives to focus on praising the One who sacrificed His. The holiness of God and His Son has been replaced with the deification of men and "little god" theology. Like those in the Old Testament who attempted to build a tower that would reach Heaven, mankind is still guilty of the oldest sin in the book— the desire to elevate ourselves to the level of our Creator.

God doesn't want us to have tunnel vision. He wants us to see the big picture, and Jesus *is* the big picture. Alistair Begg once said, "The entire Bible is a book about Jesus. Jesus is, Himself, the Gospel, the Good News. In the Old testament He's predicted, in the gospels He's revealed, in the Acts He's preached, in the Epistles He's explained, and in Revelation He's expected."

As parents and grandparents, it's important that we encourage our children, and ourselves, to look toward eternity, not just what matters to us at this moment in time. My pastor once said, "The things we put our hope in give us our most highs and our most lows. Anything can become an issue if it overly influences how we do life. Any of these good, normal, okay things can intoxicate us—can cause us to drift away from the hope and return of Jesus." There's nothing wrong with enjoying "normal, okay things" like sports, or any other number of activities, but when they take precedence over our relationship with God, then it's time to reprioritize, to look at the big picture—and the One who painted it.

Thoughts and Reflection

Spend some time reflecting on those activities that take up the bulk of your physical and mental time. Do they honor God, and are they furthering His kingdom?

Prayer

Dear heavenly Father, help me to see Your big picture. Put my priorities in an order that honors You.

Delight yourself also in the Lord, and He shall
give you the desires of your heart.
(Psalm 37:4)

THE HEART'S DESIRE

*H*ealth, wealth, and prosperity—it's the American dream. Psalm 37:4 is the go-to verse for those preaching prosperity theology. Standing in their pulpits each Sunday they distort the true gospel of Jesus Christ. They preach that it's God's will for us to be healthy and wealthy. Bethel Church in California has an offering reading that states: "We are believing the Lord for: Jobs and better jobs, raises and bonuses, benefits, sales and commissions, favorable settlements, estates and inheritances." Hmm. The congregation is "believing the Lord" for "estates and inheritances?" Sounds great, except when I read that particular phrase, the first thing that comes to mind is *somebody has to die before that happens,* which kind of puts a damper on the whole inheritance deal. Prosperity doctrines shoot straight past "Delight yourself also in the Lord," and zero in on "He shall give you the desires of your heart." In Jeremiah 17:9 the prophet points out that the heart is "deceitful above all things." If the *heart* is deceitful, then the desires of the heart are probably pretty sketchy as well. So, what *should* we desire?

[Enter Jesus]

Jesus said, "Do not lay up for yourselves treasures on earth ... but lay up for yourselves treasures in heaven ... For where your treasure is, there your heart will be also" (Matthew 6:19–21). Whatever you count as *treasure* is a reflection of your *heart,* and Jesus tells us to focus on *heavenly* treasure. So what *is* heavenly treasure? Is it pearly gates and streets of gold, or is it something more precious? The answer lies in the question—why did Jesus die? Or rather, for *whom* did He die? Jesus died for each of us—*we* are the treasure, the souls He died to save. Laying up treasures for ourselves in heaven is winning souls to Christ. What we *should* desire is furthering His kingdom.

With age comes maturity—most of the time. What we desired when we were young is rarely the same as what we desire later in life. We begin to realize that time is short, and what once seemed so important in our youth takes a back seat to the eternal. Fortunately, God knows the end from the beginning. He knows and wants what is best for us, and He hopes we will eventually want it, too. In the focus verse, when King David wrote, "He shall give you the desires of your heart," he didn't mean God will give you that fancy house, job, or sports car you've been wanting. He meant God will change, or perfect, your desires. When we delight ourselves in Him, we can be assured God will be faithful to the promise of Psalm 37:4.

So what does God want for us—or from us? "Therefore, whether you eat or drink, or whatever you do, do all to the glory of God" (1 Corinthians 10:31). God wants us to glorify Him. This is why we were created: to worship our heavenly Father. God wants us to *delight* in Him—it's that simple.

There's nothing wrong with desiring financial stability to take care of your family. In fact, the Bible says: "If anyone does not provide for his own, and especially for those of his household, he has denied the faith and is worse than an unbeliever" (1 Timothy 5:8). Money is not the problem; the *love* of money is the problem (1 Timothy 6:10). There's a reason Jesus said, "I say to you, it is easier for a camel to go through the eye of a needle than for a rich man to enter the kingdom of God" (Matthew 19:24). Unfortunately, great wealth comes with some unique obstacles—temptation, arrogance, and trusting in riches more than God.

Having money makes life easier on some level, that's for sure. However, the apostle Paul wrote, "Not that I speak in regard to need, for I have learned in whatever state I am, to be content" (Philippians 4:11). So, whether we have a lot of money, a little money, or no money, we should be content and delight in the Lord, doing everything for the glory of God.

Thoughts and Reflection

What are some things you've prayed for? Do these things glorify God? If you aren't sure, ask God to reorient your heart, so that your desires are in alignment with His.

Prayer

Dear heavenly Father, help me to want what You want for my life. Give me proper desires, desires that will glorify You and bring honor to Your name.

Moreover, when you fast, do not be like the hypocrites, with a sad countenance. For they disfigure their faces that they may appear to men to be fasting. Assuredly, I say to you, they have their reward.
(Matthew 6:16)

HYPOCRITES

*H*ave you ever known someone who was all about outward appearances, those "holier than thou" types? The Pharisees were *all* about appearances, laws, and themselves. They loved showing how virtuous they were, how holy they were, how many rules they followed, and how well they followed them. They did anything and everything they could to exalt themselves above the unwashed masses. If they were grieved or offended, they tore up their faces and ripped their clothes in dramatic fashion. When they prayed, they prayed in public to show everyone how eloquent their pleas were to the Almighty, making everyone else feel like inarticulate slugs. It's difficult to imagine living in a first-century theocracy, where the playing field was not level and all were not given the same opportunity to commune with their heavenly Father—so many rules, so many obstacles.

[Enter Jesus]

Jesus was a Pharisee's worst nightmare, a zealous rebel with a cause. He had no problem calling them what they were—hypocrites. They continually tried to trap Him yet were never successful (Matthew 19:3–9; Matthew 22:15–22; Mark 10:2–9; Luke 20:20–26). Jesus was the *opposite* of a Pharisee: They were self-righteous; He *was* righteous. They pretended to be holy; Jesus *was* holy.

The Pharisees and their counterfeit religiosity made Jesus angry, and whatever makes Jesus angry should also make us angry. So what specifically about the Pharisees angered Him? In no particular order of offense, number one: *Rules over people*. Matthew 12:1–14 cites Jesus' healing of the man with a withered hand—in the synagogue—on the Sabbath—in front of the Pharisees. They had just verbally attacked Jesus because His disciples were picking grain and eating it, which was unlawful on the Sabbath (it really wasn't, but to them it sounded like a good accusation). After He healed the man's hand, of course, they had a roundtable discussion "and plotted against Him" to "destroy Him" (Matthew 12:14).

Number two: *Judgmentalism*. Matthew 23:27 recounts Jesus telling the Pharisees that they were like beautiful, whitewashed tombs on the outside, while on the inside they were dead bones and all kinds of uncleanness—harsh, but on point. Basically, they cared more about what people saw on the outside than what was in their own hearts.

Number three: *Putting up roadblocks to God*. John 2:13–17 finds Jesus driving out the money changers in the temple. The poor had journeyed to Jerusalem for the Passover feast, following God's command. Instead of helping the people, money was being made off them. Enraged, Jesus didn't just encourage the money changers to get off His property—He *whipped* them off. Did the Pharisees make a profit, or did they simply give permission for the profit to be made by those selling animals for sacrifice? Regardless, Jesus was angry.

Number four: *Ulterior motives*. Matthew records Jesus' opinion on public praying: "And when you pray, you shall not be like the hypocrites. For they love to pray standing in the synagogues and on the corners of the streets, that they may be seen by men" (Matthew 6:5). He knew their hearts. He knew it was a show. Their motivation was not to honor God with their prayers, but to strut and gain attention for themselves.

However, before hopping onto the Pharisee-bashing bandwagon, examine their actions that angered Jesus. Are you guilty of any of them? I'm personally raising my hand on two. It's easy to look at others and say, "I'm not as bad as them," but the point is we are all bad compared to *Jesus*. We may not have been present when the religious leaders handed Him over to the Romans; however, our sins, and their sins, are *why* He was crucified.

Thoughts and Reflection

We're all hypocrites from time to time. But focus on one or two personal hang-ups that you think make God angry. Do you have a made-up set of religious rules that would keep someone from Jesus? Do you judge others, yet ignore the log in your own eye? Is anything in your behavior a roadblock to someone seeking God? Do you have ulterior motives, showing a virtuous side to the public while inwardly harboring wayward intentions?

Prayer

Dear heavenly Father, help me to desire holiness, like You are holy. Help me to identify the sins in my own life and change my thoughts and behaviors to those that are pleasing to You.

*I will contend with him who contends with
you, and I will save your children.*
(Isaiah 49:25)

BRING IT ON!

I once heard a pastor open up about some personal issues he was having. I truly admired him for that. Airing one's private laundry is never easy—especially in front of those you shepherd. He meant well, but he encouraged the congregation to call out to Satan during their own struggles and say, "Bring it on! We know who wins in the end!" Since I had experience with what he was encouraging, I thought to myself, *Nope. Nope. Nope.* A few years earlier, someone I love was wrestling with their faith. I had been praying for this person every day, asking God to restore them. The day I received a phone call and heard the words, "You won't believe this, but …" I was overjoyed. I was *so* elated I fell to my knees and thanked God. Well, not quite. What I did do was, in arrogance and pride, yell out loud to Satan, *"You just lost!"* Because obviously it was *my* prayers that brought that person back to God, right? That night I had the worst nightmare of my life. I won't get into detail, but it was terrifying. The next two days I experienced extreme unease and physical exhaustion. For the first time in my life, I had been, quite literally, spiritually attacked—and I was afraid.

[Enter Jesus]

There are hundreds of verses in the Bible telling us "fear not" and "do not be afraid," and since that day I've committed many of them to memory. There are also numerous verses about the dangers of pride. What God taught me was that it is *He*, not *me*, who is to be glorified when prayers are answered. Jude 1:9 states: "Yet Michael the archangel, in contending with the devil, when he disputed about the body of Moses, dared not bring against him a reviling accusation, but said, "The Lord rebuke you!" If the archangel Michael, the great captain of the angels, would not dare usurp God's authority, there's probably a good reason.

We do know who wins in the end, but the Bible is clear—*God* will contend with the one who contends with us. Some might ask—but hasn't God given us authority over Satan? Jesus said in Luke 10:19: "Behold, I give you the authority to trample on serpents and scorpions, and over all the power of the enemy, and nothing shall by any means hurt you." So, yes, God has given us authority, but it's not *our* authority, it's *His* authority that defeats Satan. We must always remember: "The branch cannot bear fruit of itself, unless it abides in the vine, neither can you, unless you abide in Me" (John 15:4).

Pride is a dangerous sin, and the downfall of many in the Bible: King Uzziah (2 Chronicles 26:16), King Hezekiah (2 Chronicles 32:25–26), Herod Antipas (Acts 12:21–23), and the most infamous offender of all—Satan himself (Isaiah 14:12–15).

Beyond pride, there is also the issue of tempting and testing God. For example, if I go traipsing out in the woods looking for a rattlesnake, and deliberately step on it barefooted, I'm going to get bitten—and I'm probably going to die. To expect God to protect me from something I'm doing with foolish intent is testing Him. When Jesus said, "You shall not tempt the Lord your God" in Matthew 4:7, He was speaking directly to Satan at the time, and He wasn't mincing words.

Some might argue, "What about Paul in the book of Acts? He was bitten by a snake and lived!" Acts 28:3–5 does state: "But when Paul had gathered a bundle of sticks and laid them on the fire, a viper came out because of the heat, and fastened on his hand … But he shook off the creature into the fire and suffered no harm." It's important to note that Paul was not *looking* for a snake, he was not *intentionally* provoking an incident to prove God's protective power—and neither should we.

Thoughts and Reflection

Have there been times in your life when you've tempted God? Are you always mindful that He is the One in control and that He will be the One contending with Satan for you?

Prayer

Dear heavenly Father, keep me centered on You. Remove all my fear and replace it with peace. Remove all my pride and replace it with humility. Please help me to rest in You. "The name of Lord is a strong tower; the righteous run to it and are safe" (Proverbs 18:10).

And Jesus cried out again with a loud voice, and yielded up His
spirit. Then, behold, the veil of the temple was torn in two from
top to bottom; and the earth quaked, and the rocks were split.
(Matthew 27:50–51)

BARRIERS

*F*or the Jewish people, the temple in Jerusalem was the most holy site in Israel. The first temple, built by King Solomon, was destroyed when the Babylonians laid siege to Jerusalem. The second temple was rebuilt by King Herod, but in AD 70 it was leveled to the ground by Rome, fulfilling the prophecy of Luke 21:6. The only remaining evidence of the great and holy structure is the Western Wall, a portion of the original retaining wall surrounding the Temple Mount.

The inner sanctum was called the Holy of Holies, and within it rested the Ark of the Covenant. During the Babylonian occupation of Jerusalem the Ark disappeared. When the temple was rebuilt, the Foundation Stone (a raised section of the floor) stood in place of where the Ark used to be. Yom Kippur—the day of atonement—was, and still is, the holiest day in Judaism. Once a year the high priest would enter the Holy of Holies and sprinkle a blood offering on the Mercy Seat, the golden lid placed atop the Ark of the Covenant, or onto the Foundation Stone of the second temple. The high priest would offer this blood sacrifice and ask God's forgiveness of sins committed during that past year for himself and the Jewish people (Leviticus 23:27).

The inner sanctum was twenty cubits cubed (thirty feet in length, width, and height). Separating the inner and outer sanctums was a floor-to-ceiling veil, the purpose of which was to obstruct view into the Holy of Holies. The veil was woven from blue, purple, crimson, and white thread, and though its thickness is disputed, most sources suggest it was approximately nine centimeters (slightly more than three and one-half inches). Whatever the measurement, it was dense enough to prevent anyone from seeing into the inner sanctum, where the Spirit of God dwelt among His people (Exodus 25:8–9).

[Enter Jesus]

The moment His Spirit left Him, the veil was torn—the barrier between God and His people was destroyed. *That* is why Jesus lived, died, and was resurrected—to demolish barriers and level the playing field. Unfortunately, like the veil, men have created works-based doctrines that have fashioned another barrier between God and His people. These doctrines teach that in addition to Jesus' sacrifice we must earn, or maintain, salvation by being good. Sinful man, however, can *never* be good enough. Jesus Himself said in Mark 10:18: "No one is good but One, that is God." Ephesians 2:8–9 states, "For by grace you have been saved through faith, and that not of yourselves; it is the gift of God, not of works, lest anyone should boast."

Disagreement on salvation by faith *plus* works, versus simply faith, is not new. In the book of Acts, religious leaders argued that faith plus certain customs needed to be observed for salvation (Acts 15:1). However, the apostle Peter disputed this in Acts 15:11 when he said: "But we believe that through the grace of the Lord Jesus Christ we shall be saved in the same manner as they." Good works are the *result* of salvation—not the *reason* for it.

The tearing of the veil eliminated not only a physical and symbolic barrier between God and man, but also the need for a mediator. In 1 Timothy 2:5 Paul writes: "For there is one God and one Mediator between God and men, the Man Christ Jesus." We no longer need a high priest to intercede in prayer or enter a holy place and spill sacrificial blood on our behalf. Jesus shed His blood for us; He was the spotless lamb, the perfect sacrifice.

Though some religious doctrines place emphasis on what we should *do* to earn salvation, Jesus said, "It is finished" (John 19:30). It is *done*. Because we are flawed humans, we will, unfortunately, continue to sin and need to repent, but the sacrifice of Jesus has paid for those sins—past, present, and future.

Thoughts and Reflection

Think about what you've been taught your entire life about how one gets to heaven. Are good deeds or extra prayers required? Is there biblical support for those teachings?

Prayer

Dear heavenly Father, I thank You for the gift of Jesus. Thank You that I have direct access to You for forgiveness, thanks, and worship. Help me learn more about You through Your Word each day and give me the courage to follow Your teachings.

I have heard your prayer, I have seen your tears;
surely I will add to your days fifteen years.
(Isaiah 38:5)

WHOSE WILL?

his biblical account of a king's quandary—and the wisdom required to desire God's will above our own—reminds me of a movie I saw thirty years ago, *Bill and Ted's Excellent Adventure*. The boys travel back in time to kidnap historical figures for a school report and encounter the Greek philosopher, Socrates. Uncertain as to whether he's worth "bagging," they open their history book and find this quote attributed to him: "The only true wisdom consists in knowing that you know nothing." Shocked, Ted exclaims, "That's us, dude!" That's *all* of us, Ted.

Jerusalem and King Hezekiah were in trouble. Like a swarm of locusts, the Assyrian army had swept across Israel. Now preparing to invade Jerusalem, the Assyrian king sent envoys, who delivered a message taunting Hezekiah and mocking God. The prophet Isaiah urged Hezekiah to believe in divine protection, so Hezekiah prayed. Isaiah 37:36 describes that night: "The angel of the Lord went out, and killed" 185,000 members of the Assyrian army. The Assyrian king retreated. God was faithful and delivered Jerusalem from the impending attack.

Soon after being spared from the Assyrians, Hezekiah became ill. As he lay near death, Isaiah came to him and said: "Thus says the Lord: 'Set your house in order, for you shall die and not live.'" Weeping bitterly, Hezekiah cried out to God, "Remember now, O Lord, I pray, how I have walked before You in truth … and have done what is good in Your sight" (Isaiah 38:1–3). Though God had pronounced his impending demise, because of Hezekiah's grief-stricken prayer, the Lord was merciful. Sounds great, right? Not so much.

[Enter Jesus]

Many of us have been in the place of King Hezekiah. We receive bad news and begin to bargain: *Jesus, if You will heal me I promise I will ....* Or we pray like Hezekiah prayed: *Lord, remember when I ...,* as though God needs reminding of our good deeds. King Hezekiah's story poses an interesting question for believers—how important is it to pray for God's will and not our own, in *all* things?

God is the source of true wisdom. Compared to Him we know nothing. He knows the exact moment of the last breath we will take, and, in the case of King Hezekiah, God also knew what would happen if He granted him a longer life—and He did it anyway.

But what was so terrible about the extension of King Hezekiah's life? When the king of Babylon heard Hezekiah was ill, he sent emissaries with gifts. Hezekiah, now healed, welcomed the visitors and foolishly "showed them ... all that was found among his treasures" (Isaiah 39:2). When the prophet Isaiah heard of Hezekiah's boastfulness, he declared, "Behold, the days are coming when all that is in your house ... shall be carried to Babylon ... And they shall take away some of your sons ... and they shall be eunuchs in the palace of the king of Babylon" (Isaiah 39:6–7). This was bad news for Jerusalem, and *super* bad news for Hezekiah's descendants. When Hezekiah heard Isaiah's decree, he was *so* remorseful that he fell on his face and begged God for forgiveness—but not really. His actual response was, "The word of the Lord which you have spoken is good .... At least there will be peace and truth in my days" (Isaiah 39:8).

Unfortunately, Isaiah's prophecy came to pass, and Jerusalem eventually fell to Babylon. But, before Jerusalem's prophesied destruction, Hezekiah had a son. Manasseh was a cruel king, immoral, devoted to witchcraft, and even sacrificed one of his children in the fires of Moloch worship.

Hezekiah made mistakes, but he was considered a righteous king. And yet, even with his overall desire to do God's will, when faced with death he panicked. Although it's impossible to know if Hezekiah would have accepted God's will if he had known the consequences, it gives each of us something to think about. Faced with the same deathbed scenario, would we have the wisdom or *courage* to want God's will over our own?

Thoughts and Reflection

If you knew the exact moment of your death, would your life change dramatically? If you knew the extension of your life would cause harm to others, would you have the courage to pray for God's will instead of your own?

Prayer

Dear heavenly Father, regardless of what I think is best, I don't know the end from the beginning. Help me to trust You and Your perfect timing.

For the mystery of lawlessness is already at work; only He who now restrains will do so until He is taken out of the way.
(2 Thessalonians 2:7)

RESTRAINING POWER

I have no interest in heights, natural or man-made. My pilot husband, however, loves anything tall: mountains, buildings, cliffs, dams—and, if possible, throwing things off them. One Sunday afternoon we packed up the dog and went on a long drive. Unbeknownst to me he had been planning this trip for days. He loves surprising me—I *hate* surprises. I can't count how many times I've said, "I'm not five years old. Just tell me where we're going!" He means well, and I love him for it, but I'm a planner. I need details, and lots of them. I need to know how to dress, whether to pack food, and if we should bring extra clothing.

The surprise he had in store was a hike to our county reservoir. We drove through a small town, turned down a narrow lane, and parked. It was a beautiful walk. As we approached the dam, I found the massiveness of it all quite impressive. My husband was giddy, reading every sign, hoping to find the dam's exact height, and I could see him calculating whether it was worth being caught on security camera trying to throw rocks off the top. As we got closer to the base, the immense size of the concrete structure hit us. We talked about the powerful force on the other side (the side we couldn't see yet) held back by the dam, and what would happen if it ever burst—everything below would be lost. As we walked back toward the car, my husband asked, "Did you see anything that inspired you?"

[Enter Jesus]

A dam is a structure built to hold water back and consists of many elements. At the top of the dam is a spillway, which releases excess water. Like the many elements assembled to construct a dam, God consists of many wonderful attributes. He is a "strong tower" to Whom the righteous run and are safe (Proverbs 18:10). "He is a shield to all who trust in Him" (2 Samuel 22:31). He is faithful, patient, merciful, and unchanging. Though He is currently restraining the forces of evil, like a spillway wickedness still enters the world—in mercifully controlled amounts.

Ephesians 6:12 states: "For we do not wrestle against flesh and blood, but against principalities, against powers, against the rulers of the darkness of this age, against spiritual hosts of wickedness in the heavenly places." This verse is overwhelming to me. It highlights the presence of evil all around, even though we cannot see it. Can you imagine what this world will be like once the force currently fending off evil is *taken out of the way*?

Like the warning signs posted everywhere along the reservoir cautioning people not to enter the potentially dangerous waters, the Bible tells us there will be warning signs preceding the Second Coming of Christ. There will be "wars and rumors of wars" (Matthew 24:6); "earthquakes and "famines" (Luke 21:11); and there will be false prophets who will lead people astray. Second Timothy 4:3–4 states: "For the time will come when they will not endure sound doctrine, but according to their own desires, because they have itching ears, they will heap up for themselves teachers; and they will turn their ears away from the truth, and be turned aside to fables." Jesus said many would come in His name but warns His followers not to go after them. He said, "Now when these things begin to happen, look up and lift your heads, because your redemption draws near" (Luke 21: 28).

When my husband asked if I was inspired by anything we saw I told him what was on my mind. His response was, "Wow, that's dark." And yes, for those who don't have assurance of their salvation, it *is* dark. The *good* news is that the end is not yet. Jesus is "the light of the world" and those who follow Him "shall not walk in darkness" (John 8:12). We still have time to plan, to get our souls right with God, and to lead others to Christ; but once God's mercy is *taken out of the way* there will be darkness.

Thoughts and Reflection

Are you planning for eternity the same way you plan for a day trip? If you died tomorrow, are you certain of your destination?

Prayer

Dear heavenly Father, we are surrounded by evil. Thank You for protecting my family. Please continue protecting them and prepare my heart for Your coming.

Come to Me, all you who labor and are heavy laden, and I will give you rest. Take My yoke upon you and learn from Me, for I am gentle and lowly in heart, and you will find rest for your souls. For My yoke is easy and My burden is light.
(Matthew 11:28–30)

PERMISSION TO REST

At fifty-seven, I had forgotten the challenges of finding time to rest, while caring for little ones—until last week. Our daughter and son-in-law went on a much-needed vacation, while my husband and I watched our grandchildren, ages three and six. By day two I had developed a pretty solid routine, but, because the kids are so different, I had to be creative. My husband worked long hours that week, so I was left to plan meals, take one to school for half-day kindergarten, pick him up three hours later, remember pajama day, keep the house clean, referee arguments, give baths, and still have energy for bedtime stories. The last two days, when my husband was finally home and able to help, I admittedly locked myself in the bathroom *twice* to take a long bath and listen to praise music. I went to bed when they did, got up when they did, and slept with one eye open. The day their parents picked them up I fell asleep on the couch, took a five-hour nap, then got up and went straight to bed.

In America, 46 percent of households have two full-time working parents. Moms and dads work all day, pick their children up from school or day care, fix a quick dinner, and then head off to sports or other activities. Additionally, while raising their own children, an increasing number of moms and dads are also caring for their elderly parents. With all of this, when is there time to *rest*?

[Enter Jesus]

In the book of Mark, the disciples had a lot going on as well. Jesus had been preaching in the synagogue, and, per standard procedure, He succeeded in offending people. It is recorded that "He could do no mighty work there, except that He laid His hands on a few sick people and healed them" (Mark 6:5). Later, Jesus called the twelve together. He instructed them to travel to surrounding towns, healing and preaching, and told them to take nothing for their journey except a staff—no food, no money, no extra clothes. That's a *lot* of trust for provision. During this time John the Baptist was taken into custody and beheaded. Once the disciples heard, they went and retrieved his body and laid it in a tomb. Afterward, they returned to Jesus and told Him everything they had done. "And He said to them, 'Come aside by yourselves to a deserted place and rest a while.' For there were many coming and going, and they did not even have time to eat" (Mark 6:31). No time to eat—now *that* sounds familiar, especially for busy people.

Life is hard—there's no way around it. As a parent or caregiver, you gotta do what you gotta do to take care of your family, but Jesus calls you to rest. He actually *commands* it. The fourth commandment in Genesis 2:2–3 states: "And on the seventh day God ended His work … and He rested on the seventh day …. Then God blessed the seventh day and sanctified it …." Did you see that? God Himself rested. If *He* rested, it's certain that *we* need rest. In Mark 2:27, after another Sabbath Day verbal thrashing from the Pharisees, Jesus said: "The Sabbath was made for man, and not man for the Sabbath." God created a day for us to rest and Jesus confirmed it—therefore, you have *permission to rest*.

Like all things that are good for us we must be intentional about doing them. Whether you're a parent, grandparent, or single person overwhelmed with life, whatever you have to do—putting as many heads together as you need—plan your rest. Plan at least thirty to sixty minutes of daily, duty-free time to regroup and rest your body and mind to prayerfully meditate on God's word. It will be worth the effort.

Thoughts and Reflection

Think about all you do in a day. Are there some activities you can eliminate that would give you more time with God? Keeping your children busy is important, but not at the expense of your health—or theirs.

Prayer

Dear heavenly Father, I'm so tired. I am literally exhausted. Help me to prioritize my life and create time for physical and spiritual rest, for both me and my family.

*Let the little children come to Me, and do not forbid
them; for of such is the kingdom of heaven.
(Matthew 19:14)*

PRECIOUS IN HIS SIGHT

O ur grandson's vocabulary is pretty mature for a six-year-old, and at times catches me completely off guard. While watching *Finding Nemo* with him I was trying to build up a scene. I said, "Uh oh! That light is bad news for Marlin and Dory!" Without missing a beat he replied, "It's an Anglerfish, Mamaw. They use the light to attract their prey." Well, alrighty then.

Our son's vocabulary wasn't quite as impressive at five, but one evening, while lying on our bed watching cartoons with his sister, he said something beyond his years. He asked, "Mom, if you had been alive when Jesus was alive, would you have voted to let Him go?" I was taken aback by this question from a five-year-old, but said, "Of course I would!" He agreed, then, after a long pause, said, "I changed my mind. I would have voted for Barnabas (Barabbas)." A little stunned, I asked why. He said, "I would vote for Barnabas, because if Jesus didn't die, we couldn't go to Heaven." Out of the mouths of babes.

[Enter Jesus]

In Matthew 19, Jesus and His disciples had departed Galilee for Judea. He was followed by multitudes of people wanting to hear Him speak—and Pharisees seeking to trap Him in His words. Among the crowd of people were parents who wanted Jesus to lay hands on, and pray for, their children. The disciples, however, reprimanded them. What was up with that? As far as we know Simon Peter was the only married disciple and we don't know whether he had any children, so maybe it was a "Stop bothering the Savior" kind of moment. But Jesus said, "Let the little children come to Me, and do not forbid them; for of such is the kingdom of heaven" (Matthew 19:14).

What does "for of such is the kingdom of heaven" mean? Obviously, heaven won't be populated only by children, but *obviously,* Jesus meant something significant. In the previous chapter the disciples asked Jesus who would be the *greatest* in the kingdom of heaven. Jesus called to a little child and sat him in the middle of the disciples and said, "Assuredly, I say to you, unless you are converted and become as little children, you will by no means enter the kingdom of heaven. Therefore whoever humbles himself as this little child is the greatest in the kingdom of heaven" (Matthew 18:3-4). It's all about attitude—humility. Children are too innocent to be arrogant; that nasty quality develops over time.

Our children are precious to us. How much more precious do you think they are to God? In Matthew 18:6, Jesus said: "But whoever causes one of these little ones who believe in Me to sin, it would be better for him if a millstone were hung around his neck, and he were drowned in the depth of the sea." These words should send chills down the spine of any individual, school district, or entertainment corporation that intentionally leads children away from God.

Our world is a frustrating place. There is so much evil, and much of the time it appears children are the target. As parents, grandparents, and church leaders it is our duty to "Train up a child in the way he should go, and when he is old he will not depart from it" (Proverbs 22:6).

Unfortunately, a proverb is not a promise. A proverb is the way life *usually* goes; it is not an assurance from God. Most of us know someone who walked away from the life for which his parents had hoped, or a rebel who refused to march to the beat of her Christian parents' drum. But if we don't teach our children to follow Christ, who will? Yes, eventually they will make their own decisions, and at that point we are released from responsibility—except to pray for their return to Him.

Thoughts and Reflection

Are you spending as much time teaching your children about Jesus as you are teaching them to excel in academics, sports, or musical instruments? The chance they will become a professional athlete or musician is minuscule, but that they will one day meet Jesus is a certainty. Are you training them in the way they should go?

Prayer

Dear heavenly Father, help me to raise my children in Your way, to dedicate as much time teaching them about You and Your Word as I do about things in this life that, in the big picture, don't matter at all.

The Lord is near to those who have a broken heart,
and saves such as have a contrite spirit.
(Psalm 34:18)

WHY?

I wrote "Why?" weeks ago but revised the opening paragraph after learning that a second member of our church passed away this morning. The songs chosen by the worship team were two of my favorites. Unfortunately, I could not "Raise a Hallelujah," even though I knew there was joy in the "House of the Lord." I am not yet at the level of spiritual maturity where I can immediately rejoice when a soul passes from this life into the next, even if I am confident of that person's salvation. Most of us have experienced the loss of a loved one, and in our moment of greatest despair we've cried out to God, "*Why?*" Broken hearts are left in the wake of death, and families are forced to pick up the pieces of a life they're not even sure they want to live anymore.

[Enter Jesus]

So why does God allow bad things to happen to good people? I was directed to an answer this morning, and the truth is that only once in the history of the world has something *bad* ever happened to someone *good*. Jesus said in Luke 18:19: "No one is good but One, that is, God." The only good person ever to have lived was Jesus, who willingly suffered an excruciating and undeserved death—for us.

While preaching the Sermon on the Mount Jesus said, "He makes His sun rise on the evil and on the good, and sends rain on the just and on the unjust" (Matthew 5:45). As evil as Hitler was, he, too, was allowed to experience beauty, happiness, and laughter. That's probably not the way I would have dealt with Hitler if I were

God—but I'm not God. He is the Creator, and the Creator is allowed to define His creation.

In my search for answers, I was led to Isaiah 57:1–2, which states: "The righteous perishes, and no man takes it to heart; merciful men are taken away, while no one considers that the righteous is taken away from evil. He shall enter into peace; they shall rest in their beds, each one walking in his uprightness." Even though the loss of a loved one is heartbreaking, could it be they are being spared from something more painful in the future?

This verse in Isaiah caused me to think about my own father's death. As painful as it is to remember how cancer destroyed my once strong and stubborn dad, I have comfort in knowing that he is in heaven. What would have been unbearable is being in doubt of where he was going to spend eternity. Could it be God spared him from an event in the future that would have caused him, or us, more pain?

As compassionate humans it's difficult to see the wicked prosper and the innocent struggle; to know children are starving or being abused; to know that our loved ones are suffering. It doesn't seem fair. But God has not promised us an easy life. In fact, Philippians 1:29 states: "For to you it has been granted on behalf of Christ, not only to believe in Him, but also to suffer for His sake." Paul states in 2 Timothy 3:12: "Yes, and all who desire to live godly in Christ Jesus will suffer persecution." Nobody likes the idea of suffering, but it is impossible for us to be made into the image of Christ without it.

We've all heard the cliché, "no pain, no gain." Though physiologically untrue, because pain is an indication something is wrong, the phrase is certainly tossed around a lot. It would be more accurate to say "If you aren't pushed to your limits, you will never grow"—but that neither flows well nor rhymes. The point is, if we never experienced hardship, it would be impossible to grow spiritually. We learn patience through situations that inherently cause impatience. We learn to forgive by being betrayed. We learn not to gossip by hearing secrets and keeping them to ourselves. And we learn to depend upon Jesus when there's no strength left within ourselves.

Thoughts and Reflection

In an upside-down world, where bad people seem to thrive and decent people suffer, how can you make a difference? How can you reflect God's love to someone who is hurting and without hope?

Prayer

Dear heavenly Father, teach me how to pray for the brokenhearted. Give me Your strength when I am weak, and Your wisdom when I don't know what to do or what to say.

Therefore let us not judge one another anymore,
but rather resolve this, not to put a stumbling block
or a cause to fall in our brother's way.
(Romans 14:13)

ROCKY ROADS

*W*hen I think of a stumbling block, I think of a stone slightly raised from the ground just waiting for that unsuspecting foot—usually mine. I'm relatively accident prone, so if there's anything to trip over, I'm going to trip over it. Then again, sometimes I lose my footing, only to realize there was absolutely nothing in the way except my own lack of gracefulness. Life can be like that. We can be our own worst enemy, tripping over our own two feet. What we do *not* want is to be the cause for another poor soul to trip and fall on their face.

Unfortunately, what *we* see as a few small stones may be viewed as a path-diverting obstacle for another. A road paved with cobblestones is no problem for someone wearing appropriate footwear. But for a person in a wheelchair, it's a path impossible to navigate, causing them to change course altogether.

[Enter Jesus]

Matthew records Jesus and His disciples once again being pursued by the Pharisees. This time they wanted Jesus to show them a sign—of course they did. But He said to them: "A wicked and adulterous generation seeks after a sign, and no sign shall be given to it except the sign of the prophet Jonah" (Matthew 16:4). Jesus declaring that the only sign He would give them was the "sign of Jonah" probably didn't help His standing in the eyes of the Pharisees. Jonah was in the belly of the great fish for three days before being spit up on shore. Likewise, Jesus would be in the tomb for three days, then resurrected to life. That the Pharisees were familiar with Jonah was a given. That Jesus would die and be resurrected, however, would never be within their scope of spiritual understanding.

In Matthew 16:13–16, Jesus and the disciples approached Caesarea Philippi. He asked them, "Who do men say that I, the Son of Man, am?" They replied that the names of Elijah, John the Baptist, Jeremiah, or one of the other prophets were being tossed around. He then asked, "But who do you say that I am?" Simon Peter replied, "You are the Christ, the Son of the living God." Afterward, Jesus instructed his disciples not to tell anyone that He was the Messiah—then the conversation took a turn.

After Peter's pronouncement, Jesus began to speak of His own fate. He told the disciples that He would go to Jerusalem and suffer at the hands of the chief priests, and that He would ultimately die but be resurrected on the third day. Simon Peter pulled Him aside and basically said, *no way, no how* is this going to happen to You! To which Jesus replied, "Get behind me, Satan! You are an offense to Me; for you are not mindful of the things of God, but the things of man" (Matthew 16:21–23). Simon Peter, the *first* disciple to recognize Christ's divinity, was essentially called a satanic stumbling block for attempting to divert Jesus from what He had been born to do—and it stuck with him. In 1 Peter 5:8 he writes: "Be sober, be vigilant; because your adversary the devil walks about like a roaring lion, seeking whom he may devour."

In Luke 17:1, Jesus said to his disciples: "It is impossible that no offenses should come, but woe to him through whom they do come!" A stumbling block is a metaphor for a behavior or attitude that could lead someone to corrupt behavior. For example, someone who professes Christ as their Savior may be able to drink wine without any problem (in moderation, not allowing for drunkenness). However, if a Christian drinks wine around someone who believes drinking is a sin (or is an alcoholic), which leads *them* to begin drinking, that Christian has become a stumbling block to them. Like Simon Peter stated, we must be sober-minded and watchful at all times, ensuring Satan does not use us to turn someone away from Jesus.

Thoughts and Reflection

What someone else views as sin may not be a sin to you. It's possible that your spiritual maturity (your appropriate footwear) allows you to participate in activities that another finds objectionable. Make sure your motivations are always pure and in line with God's Word.

Prayer

Dear heavenly Father, help me to always be mindful of another's struggles. Prevent me from doing anything that would stand in their way or obstruct their path to You.

Have you not made a hedge around him, around his household,
and around all that he has on every side? You have blessed the
work of his hands, and his possessions have increased in the land.
(Job 1:10)

HEDGES

*H*ave you ever heard someone pray for a hedge of protection? I used to pray this specifically for my family every day, and then one morning I asked myself—what good is a hedge? In *my* neighborhood a hedge is a row of arborvitae trees. If you want to protect someone, a row of flimsy ferns doesn't seem like the way to go no matter how large they are. So I began praying for a shield. I then realized that a shield doesn't really guard from behind. I now pray for a *sphere* of protection—I figure that will cover every physical or spiritual attack from up, down, and all around. One evening I asked my mother-in-law her thoughts on hedges of protection, and whether she thought a hedge was the best form of defense. She replied, "Well, I guess it depends on what's in the hedge."

[Enter Jesus]

In ancient Israel, hedges weren't simply rows of delicate bushes; they weren't even fences. Hedges were stone walls enveloped by tangled, sharp, thorny shrubs that grew around what needed protecting. Today, we have various forms of safeguards for our families: locks on our doors, deadbolts on main entryways, privacy fences, hidden cameras, dogs, security systems, and weapons. In Luke 11:21–22, Jesus said: "When a strong man, fully armed, guards his own palace, his goods are in peace." Sounds great, but then He says in verse 22: "But when a stronger than he comes upon him and overcomes him, he takes from him all his armor in which he trusted, and divides his spoils."

There is nothing wrong with taking security precautions, but consider King David when he was a young shepherd boy. King Saul's men, including David's brothers, were fighting for Israel against the Philistines. David was sent by his father to take food to his brothers. When he arrived at the Israelite camp, he rushed to the battle lines to speak to them. The Philistines thought they had an ace in the hole with Goliath. Standing nine feet tall, defiantly yelling at the army of Saul, he must have been a horrific sight to the average soldier. King Saul heard reports of the young boy at the front line and sent for him. David boldly said to the king, "Let no man's heart fail because of him; your servant will go and fight with this Philistine" (1 Samuel 17:32). Saul reluctantly agreed to let David fight the giant and dressed him in his own personal armor. Being so small, David didn't have the strength to maneuver around in the king's heavy battle gear, so he took it off, went to the brook, picked up five smooth stones, and headed toward Goliath.

I'm sure David was quite a spectacle as he approached the experienced soldier. That a boy would dare challenge him was the greatest of insults, and Goliath said to David, "Am I a dog, that you come to me with sticks?" David then said to the Philistine, "You come to me with a sword, with a spear, and with a javelin. But I come to you in the name of the Lord of hosts … This day the Lord will deliver you into my hand, and I will strike you and take your head from you … that all the earth may know that there is a God in Israel" (1 Samuel 17:43–46). We know what happened next—David took a single stone from his pouch, placed it in his sling, slung it at the giant, and killed him.

David didn't have a shield, he didn't have physical body armor, and he *knew* Goliath was stronger and could overpower him. All he had was a sling, some stones, and his faith in God. We have our own versions of slings and stones in the twenty-first century, but our ultimate protection lies in the power of our heavenly Father. In the words of King David: "You will revive me; You will stretch out

Your hand against the wrath of my enemies, and Your right hand will save me" (Psalm 138:7).

Thoughts and Reflection

Do you depend more on your limited ability to protect your loved ones, or do you depend more upon God?

Prayer

Dear heavenly Father, take my sling and my stones and direct them however You will to protect my family, but give me the ability to turn their safety completely over to You.

Honor your father and your mother, that your days may be long upon the land which the Lord your God is giving you. (Exodus 20:12)

OBEDIENCE

*D*isobedience is inherent. It's part of sinful human nature. We don't have to be taught disobedience; it's as natural as breathing. We have to be taught obedience. Raising children who respect and honor their parents can be challenging, but it's a worthwhile investment of time and effort.

One of the most remarkable acts of obedience in the Bible takes place in the book of Daniel. When Jerusalem fell to Babylon, the Jewish people were taken into captivity and forced to acclimate to the Babylonian lifestyle. Shadrach, Meshach, and Abed-Nego were respected Jewish men within the empire, yet maintained their faithfulness to God despite the Babylonian influence. Life was going along pretty well until King Nebuchadnezzar ordered the construction of a golden image in his likeness, commanding everyone in Babylon to worship it. Failure to do so would result in a horrific, fiery death.

The three young men refused to conform, and when called before Nebuchadnezzar, they bravely stood firm. They told the king, "Our God whom we serve is able to deliver us from the burning fiery furnace, and He will deliver us from your hand, O king. But if not, let it be known to you, O king, that we do not serve your gods, nor will we worship the gold image which you have set up" (Daniel 3:17–18). And so Nebuchadnezzar followed through with the penalty. In his anger, he ordered the furnace to be heated seven times hotter than usual, and as a result the flames killed the soldiers who threw the three young men into the fire.

[Enter Jesus]

After Shadrach, Meshach, and Abed-Nego were cast into the fiery furnace, something miraculous happened. Daniel 3:24–25 recounts Nebuchadnezzar saying to his counselors: "Did we not cast three men bound into the midst of the fire? …. I see four men loose … and the form of the fourth is like the Son of God." The young men walked out of the furnace unharmed, and as a result the king issued a decree that no one was to speak against their God "because there is no other God who can deliver like this" (Daniel 3:29). There was another in the fire, but did Nebuchadnezzar see Jesus or did he see an angel? Whoever it was, He was there by God's authority.

Another Godly example of a child honoring His mother was Jesus Himself. John records Jesus attending a wedding in the city of Cana. "And when they ran out of wine, the mother of Jesus said to Him, "They have no wine" (John 2:3). Although it isn't documented that Mary specifically *asked* Jesus to help with the situation, it's sufficiently implied, because after His mother's announcement Jesus did, in fact, turn water into wine—His first miracle. He was a man, the Son of God, yet *still* obeyed His mother.

In a generation where discipline and punishment are frowned upon, being a godly parent is tough. Being consistent and following through with discipline is downright exhausting. Frankly, it's easier to give in. But Proverbs 13:24 states: "He who spares his rod hates his son, but he who loves him disciplines him promptly." To be clear, "sparing the rod" does not mean "failing to beat" your children—it means failing to *discipline* them. We need look no further than the national news to see the result of parents failing to discipline their children—individuals who have no respect for authority.

Exodus 20:12 is my favorite verse regarding honoring fathers and mothers. It isn't just the fifth commandment; it's the only commandment with a promise, and explains *why* children need to obey—so that they will live longer lives. Though there is no guarantee of an extended trouble-free life, God's commandments, like parental rules, are meant to protect His children. Jeremiah 29:11 states: "For I know the thoughts I think toward you, says the Lord, thoughts of peace and not of evil, to give you a future and a hope."

Thoughts and Reflection

Obedience isn't just for children. Jesus said in John 15:14: "You are my friends if you do whatever I command you." If you are a child of God, His Holy Spirit is prompting you to follow His commands.

Prayer

Dear heavenly Father, help me to be a godly parent and a faithful servant. Give me the strength and stamina to do what is right, reflecting Your love to my child and to others. Help me to put what is *best* in front of what is *easiest*.

But those who wait on the Lord shall renew their strength.
They shall mount up with wings like eagles; they shall
run and not be weary, they shall walk and not faint.
(Isaiah 40:31)

HOPE

According to the World Health Organization, "Over 700,000 people die due to suicide every year, and it's the fourth leading cause of death in 15–29 year olds," (Suicide-WHO World Health Organization-June 17, 2021). That's quite a disturbing statistic. The last couple of years have been devastating on every level, including mental health. Countries have suffered economically, and families have been torn apart either by death, illness, or disagreement. However, depression is not new; it is as old as the world itself. I'm certain Adam and Eve were pretty discouraged after being cast out of the Garden of Eden. They went from perfection to desolation, from *no* pain to all kinds of pain. And worst of all, from communion *with* God to separation *from* God.

> King David experienced hopelessness: "For my iniquities have gone over my head; like a heavy burden they are too heavy for me" (Psalm 38:4).

> The prophet Elijah was despondent: "It is enough! Now, Lord, take my life, for I am no better than my fathers!" (1 Kings 19:4).

> Jonah was so angry he wanted to die: "Lord, please take my life from me, for it is better for me to die than to live!" (Jonah 4:3).

> And then there's Job—he had it all, lost it all, and felt despair: "Why did I not die at birth?" (Job 3:11).

[Enter Jesus]

Jesus Himself experienced despair like no other before or after Him. He was prophesied to be "a man of sorrows and acquainted with grief" (Isaiah 53:3). In the Garden of Gethsemane, He prayed: "O My Father, if it is possible, let this cup pass from Me" (Matthew 26:39). He was in such anguish that "His sweat became like great drops of blood falling down to the ground" (Luke 22:44). I cannot fathom anxiety so severe that it would cause blood to seep from the pores of my skin (hematohidrosis).

There are many reasons for despair and hopelessness: loss of income, illness, abuse, divorce—the list is endless. Even those who seem to weather all kinds of bad with a smile on their face and joy in their heart will find themselves in despair at some point. So what does the Bible say about hope? King David wrote in Psalm 71:5: "For You are my hope, O Lord God, You are my trust from my youth." Hebrews 6:19 states: "This hope we have as an anchor of the soul, both sure and steadfast." And the hope of all hopes in John 3:16: "For God so loved the world, that He gave His only begotten Son, that whoever believes in Him should not perish, but have everlasting life." *Jesus* is our eternal hope.

Feelings of depression and hopelessness may be transitory, or they may be an ongoing condition. Unfortunately, some within the religious community associate depression with sin or lack of faith. Following that rationale, all illness would be a result of sin or lack of faith. Situational depression can be temporary; however, chronic depression needs to be evaluated and treated. It is not weakness to seek help for something you cannot control. I suffered from postpartum depression after my son was born. Fortunately, a dear friend encouraged me to seek treatment—otherwise, I shudder to think what might have happened.

All illness and death are the result of original sin. "Therefore, just as through one man sin entered into the world, and death through sin, and thus death spread to all men" (Romans 5:12). We are told in scripture that in this life there will be trials and tribulation. Scripture also tells us that one day "God will wipe away every tear from their eyes; there shall be no more death, nor sorrow, nor crying. There shall be no more pain, for the former things have passed away" (Revelation 21:4). And there, dear reader, is where our eternal hope lies.

Thoughts and Reflection

If you are having ongoing feelings of hopelessness, in addition to seeking God, please contact a crisis help center or depression hotline. If you know someone who is experiencing depression, help them take those first steps to healing.

Prayer

Dear heavenly Father, help me place my hope in You and not my circumstances. My circumstances will change, You will not. Lift me up and surround me with Your love and a sense of peace that only You can provide. Help me to be an encouragement to someone else who is suffering from lost hope.

*Be diligent to present yourself approved to God, a worker who
does not need to be ashamed, rightly dividing the word of truth.
(2 Timothy 2:15)*

TRUTH OR PERCEPTION?

*I*s truth subjective or objective? *Subjective* truth is based on one's perspective, opinions, and feelings. *Objective* truth is based on reality; what exists and can be verified. Take the case of Nicholas Sandmann. In January 2019 there was a confrontation between Covington Catholic students and other demonstrators near the Lincoln Memorial. A viral video showed what appeared to be a "smirking" Sandmann standing in front of Native American activist, Nathan Phillips. Initial reports indicated the students were the aggressors. However, after some genuine fact finding, it was determined that a group of Black Hebrew Israelites had been taunting the students by hurling racial epithets and homophobic slurs. The students retaliated with school spirit chants, while dancing to the beat of Nathan Phillips's drum.

Before the truth was revealed, a news host tweeted to his followers, "Have you ever seen a more punchable face than this kid's?" Due to what was *perceived* to be smirking, the sixteen-year-old received death threats and his reputation was damaged. Later, when asked about the "smirk," Sandmann said, "I see it as a smile, saying that this is the best you're going to get out of me. You won't get any further reaction of aggression. And I'm willing to stand here as long as you want to hit this drum in my face" (nbcnews. com). Getting the truth right is critical, but in a world filled with self-absorbed humans peddling individual truths, it's becoming harder to find.

[Enter Jesus]

In John 14:6, Jesus said: "I am the way, the truth, and the life. No one comes to the Father except through Me." Jesus is the truth, and He is the only bridge between mankind and God. He warned the people of deceivers who would come to them dressed in sheep's clothing, saying, "Many will say to me in that day, 'Lord, Lord, have we not prophesied in Your name, cast out demons in Your name, and done many wonders in Your name?' And then I will declare to them, 'I never knew you; depart from Me, you who practice lawlessness!'" (Matthew 7:22–23). Can you imagine hearing these condemning words being directed at you while standing before Jesus? This is why getting the truth right is so important.

If truth is *so* important, how can we be certain the words contained within scripture are true? First, Paul writes that "All Scripture is given by inspiration of God, and is profitable for doctrine, for reproof, for correction, for instruction in righteousness, that the man of God may be complete, thoroughly equipped for every good work" (2 Timothy 3:16–17). Second, the Bible we have today consists of sixty-six separate books and was written by more than forty authors, most of whom did not know each other. Over a span of fifteen hundred years, these divinely inspired words were assembled by shepherds, fishermen, prophets, priests, and kings. It is simply implausible that this perfectly cohesive manuscript came together without divine intervention.

Adding to its credibility, the Bible is laden with fulfilled prophecies. Twenty-six hundred years prior to World War II, the prophet Isaiah wrote: "Instead of a sweet smell there will be a stench; instead of a sash, a rope; instead of well-set hair, baldness; instead of a rich robe, a girding of sackcloth; and branding instead of beauty" (Isaiah 3:24). This is a shocking visual, but accurate to the Jewish experience during the Holocaust. Additionally, in 1948, the United Nations declared Israel a state. Jews from all over the world began their journey home—fulfilling a twenty-five-hundred-year-old prophecy by the prophet Jeremiah. To Israel, God says: "I will bring you back from your captivity; I will gather you from all the nations and from all the places where I have driven you, says the Lord" (Jeremiah 29:14).

"If we say that we have fellowship with Him, and walk in darkness, we lie and do not practice the truth" (1 John 1:6). Sadly, we are all guilty of lying. It's a form of self-preservation—just ask any child desperate to get out of trouble. But, when you desire to live a life pleasing to God above everything else, "the truth shall make you free" (John 8:32).

Thoughts and Reflection

Do you believe subjective and objective truth can coexist? How can *real* "truth" be determined if everyone has their *own* "truth"?

Prayer

Dear heavenly Father, give me wisdom and discernment as I navigate this life. Help me to firmly rest on Your promises and in Your perfect truth.

Jesus said to him, "I am the way, the truth, and the life.
No one comes to the Father except through Me."
(John 14:6)

LIAR, LUNATIC, OR LEGIT?

Nearly every major belief system recognizes His existence, and their acknowledgments pose an interesting question. But first, let's look at each religion's perspective on Jesus.

According to *Cold-Case Christianity* by J. Warner and Jimmy Wallace, Judaism believes Jesus was the son of Mary. He was a teacher, had many disciples, was respected, performed miracles, claimed to be the Messiah, was crucified, and that the tomb was found empty. Judaism does not, however, acknowledge the resurrection.

Islam believes Jesus was born of a virgin. He was a prophet, a wise teacher, and He performed miracles. He ascended to Heaven, and He will return again.

Hinduism believes Jesus was a holy man, a wise teacher, and a god.

Buddhism believes Jesus was enlightened, a wise teacher, and a holy man.

The New Age movement believes Jesus was a wise, moral teacher.

[Enter Jesus]

If major religions have statements of belief in His existence, it would be wise to learn more about this Jesus. Therefore, we will examine seven claims Jesus made about *Himself*:

1. *Son of God/Son of Man*. In Matthew 26:63–64, the high priest demanded for Jesus to tell them if He was the Son of God. Jesus answered by saying, "It is as you said. Nevertheless, I say to you, hereafter you will see the Son of Man sitting at the right hand of the Power, and coming on the clouds of heaven."

2. *Giver of eternal life*. "I give them eternal life, and they shall never perish; neither shall anyone snatch them out of My hand" (John 10:28).

3. *One with the Father*. "I and My Father are one" (John 10:30).

4. *Able to forgive sins*. "The Son of Man has power on earth to forgive sins" (Matthew 9:6).

5. *The great I Am*. "Most assuredly, I say to you, before Abraham was, I AM" (John 8:58).

6. *The Messiah*. When Jesus encountered the Samaritan woman at the well, she said, "When He [the Messiah] comes, He will tell us all things." Jesus said to her, "I who speak to you am He" (John 4:25–26).

7. *The future judge*. "For the Father judges no one, but has committed all judgment to the Son, that all should honor the Son just as they honor the Father. He who does not honor the Son does not honor the Father who sent Him" (John 5:22–23).

Giver of eternal life, one with God, the Messiah, the Son of God, forgiver of sins, and future judge are some pretty audacious claims. So, I pose this question: How can someone who made these statements be considered moral, wise, and holy—if He was lying? Or perhaps Jesus was a lunatic? Other religions, and even some "Christians," want to cherry pick what they believe about Jesus, but He either *is* or is *not* who He claimed to be.

To paraphrase C.S. Lewis: You can call Him a fool, you can disparage Him and murder Him as one of Satan's demons; or you can humbly bow before Him and declare Him Lord. But let's not approach this subject with any lofty absurdities about Jesus simply being a wise, moral, and respected human teacher. He has not left that topic open for discussion, and He had no intention of doing so. As for myself, I know what I believe and why I believe it, and it is clear to me that Jesus was neither a lunatic nor a liar. And, no matter how terrifying or improbable it may seem, I wholeheartedly cling to the belief that He *was* and *is* God. As for those who *don't* believe, "Even the demons believe—and tremble" (James 2:19).

Thoughts and Reflection

Jesus' claims are either truths, lies, or the tirades of a madman. For those still struggling to believe, consider nonbiblical written sources for Jesus' existence: Flavius Josephus, a first-century Romano-Jewish historian; Tacitus, a Roman historian and senator; letters of Pliny the Younger to Emperor Trajan; evidence from the Babylonian Talmud; writings from Lucian of Samosata, a second century Greek satirist; the writings of Thallus, a Pagan historian, as referenced by Julius Africanus; and Eusebius of Caesarea, a Greek historian of Christianity.

Prayer

Dear heavenly Father, thank You for Your Son, Jesus. Thank You for His sacrifice. I know I am not alone when I suffer, at times, from unbelief. I pray in those moments of human weakness, like the man who brought his son to Jesus for healing, "Lord, I believe; help my unbelief!" (Mark 9:24).

I will give you a new heart and put a new spirit within you; I will take
the heart of stone out of your flesh and give you a heart of flesh.
(Ezekiel 36:26)

DOING A 180

S aul of Tarsus was a Roman citizen, a Pharisee, and was greatly feared. He was basically in charge of tracking down Christians and throwing them into jail (Acts 22:5). In his mind, followers of the crucified rabbi from Nazareth embodied a false and dangerous belief system that threatened traditional Judaism.

Stephen, one of Christ's followers, was dragged before the Jewish elders and accused of blasphemy. He stood before them "full of faith and power," and "they were not able to resist the wisdom and the Spirit by which he spoke" (Acts 6:8–10). After giving an eloquent account of God's promises to Abraham, Joseph's rise to power, and Moses leading the Israelites out of Egypt, Stephen admonished the high priest and said in Acts 7:51–52: "You stiff-necked and uncircumcised in heart and ears! You always resist the Holy Spirit; as your fathers did … Which of the prophets did your fathers not persecute? And they killed those who foretold the coming of the Just One, of whom you now have become the betrayers and murderers."

Not surprisingly, when the religious leaders heard this, they were beside themselves with anger. But, Stephen, filled with the Holy Spirit, gazed into heaven, and proclaimed to everyone that he saw "the heavens opened and the Son of Man standing at the right hand of God!" (Acts 7:56). At this point the self-righteous leaders lost all control, ran at him, dragged him out of the city, and, laying their clothes at the feet of Saul, stoned Stephen to death, making him the first Christian martyr.

As for Saul, he wreaked havoc within the church, storming into houses, and "dragging off men and women, committing them to prison" (Acts 8:3). Saul appeared to be a hardhearted lost cause, but when God has a plan for someone's life, He will give them a new heart and miraculously make a way—*His* way.

[Enter Jesus]

Accompanied by an entourage, Saul planned to continue his reign of terror in Damascus, intending to arrest more followers of Jesus and bring them back to Jerusalem. While he was on his way to the city, Acts 9:3–5 says "Suddenly a light shone around him from heaven. Then he fell to the ground, and heard a voice saying to him, "Saul, Saul, why are you persecuting Me?" Saul asked, "Who are You, Lord?" Then the Lord said, "I am Jesus, whom you are persecuting."

After this mind-blowing experience, the life of Saul of Tarsus flipped 180 degrees. Following his life-changing, come-to-Jesus moment, Saul was blinded. His companions led him to Damascus, where he didn't eat or drink for three days. In the meantime, Jesus appeared in a vision to the disciple, Ananias, and told him to go and find Saul. Ananias was obviously hesitant, because news of Saul's cruelty had spread. But Jesus reassured him by saying, "Go, for he is a chosen vessel of Mine." So Ananias went to Saul and said, "The Lord Jesus, who appeared to you … has sent me that you may receive your sight and be filled with the Holy Spirit." Saul regained his sight immediately, "and he arose and was baptized" (Acts 9:15–8). Saul went from brutal bad guy to believer—in three days.

Saul wasn't the only one who did a 180. Prior to Jesus' crucifixion the disciples seemed steadfast and confident. However, in the Garden of Gethsemane, when faced with an angry multitude carrying weapons, "the disciples forsook Him and fled" (Matthew 26:56). Though they initially fell victim to fear, after Jesus' resurrection they were emboldened. Just before He ascended to heaven, Jesus commanded His disciples to remain in Jerusalem and promised them the comforter would come. At Pentecost, the disciples received the Holy Spirit, and from that day forward they boldly proclaimed the gospel of Christ—*without* fear.

A personal encounter with Jesus produces change, whether instant or gradual. If Jesus can alter the lives of the disciples and Paul in such a radical way, imagine what He can do for you.

Thoughts and Reflection

How did your life change after accepting Jesus as your Savior? Did you immediately receive a new heart, or has the change been a more gradual one?

Prayer

Dear heavenly Father, thank You for Your Son, Jesus, and the continual changes He is making in my life. Thank You for Your Holy Spirit, who guides me and leads me in the way I should go.

Do you not know that those who run In a race all run, but one
receives the prize? Run in such a way that you may obtain it.
(1 Corinthians 9:24)

THE ULTIMATE RACE

*W*hen my grandson was four years old, my daughter received a phone call from his preschool—the call you don't want to get. An outdoor obstacle course had been set up for the kids, with varying levels of difficulty. When time came for *his* race, my grandson mounted the tricycle and sped away. Before long he realized he was going to lose. He stopped peddling, got off his assigned three-wheeler, ran over to his competitor—and pushed him off. This behavior, of course, received negative feedback from everyone, especially his parents. A few days later I asked him why he pushed the other child off the tricycle. Without hesitation he replied, "Because I wanted to win." Unlike his *behavior*, his *reply* received mixed reviews. Some were mortified, a few thought it was hilarious (especially his uncle), but one of my coworkers thought it was impressive—impressive because of my grandson's honesty and shameless desire to win. Nevertheless, I'm pretty sure physically disabling your opponent is not what the apostle Paul meant when he told his followers to "run in such a way" as to obtain the prize.

[Enter Jesus]

Jesus and his disciples had just left the temple in Jerusalem, when Jesus prophesied its destruction: "Not one stone shall be left here upon another." He went on to describe what the end of days would look like: "Wars and rumors of wars ... famines, pestilences, and earthquakes in various places. All these are the beginning of sorrows" (Matthew 24:2–8). On a personal note, He told the disciples they would endure difficulty, death, and be hated for His name's sake. Their lives, their individual *races*, were not going to be easy.

The key to any successful race is preparation. For an athlete, strengthening the body is essential; exercise, plenty of sleep, and a healthy diet. Maintaining good habits is important, but equally important is getting rid of harmful ones. Paul says: "Let us lay aside every weight, and the sin which so easily ensnares us, and let us run with endurance the race that is set before us" (Hebrews 12:1). Like a physical race, running our life race well requires us to strengthen ourselves spiritually and eliminate those things—those sins—that easily entangle us, preventing us from living a life that honors God.

Beyond physical preparation, an athlete must heed the instruction of a trusted coach. When the athlete adheres to guidance provided by someone who has already been there and done that, there's a greater chance for success. Jesus *has* been there. He *knows* what it is to suffer. For Christians, submitting ourselves to God, desiring His will above our own, results in a victorious, Spirit-filled life. But we're human, and there will be times when we deviate from the path God has for us. Thankfully, Jesus' sacrifice enables us to ask forgiveness when we go astray. All we have to do is ask Him for redirection to get us back on course.

In a world filled with sin, staying on God's path can be challenging, so we have to be on guard. Paul says in Galatians 5:7–9: "You ran well. Who hindered you from obeying the truth? This persuasion does not come from Him who calls you. A little leaven leavens the whole lump." God does not hinder Christians from obeying the truth—Satan does. Through Satan's influence, sin and corruption (leaven) creep into our lives. Unless we're vigilant, a little sin can easily overpower us.

Life is hard, but the good news is we have a Helper, the Holy Spirit, who will walk with us in difficult circumstances. Romans 5:3–4 tells us: "Glory in tribulations, knowing that tribulation produces perseverance." Regarding life's difficulties, James 1:12 states: "Blessed is the man who endures temptation; for when he has been approved, he will receive the crown of life which the Lord has promised to those who love Him." Ultimately, when our time on earth is over, we want to stand before God and be able to say, "I have fought the good fight, I have finished the race, I have kept the faith" (2 Timothy 4:7).

Thoughts and Reflection

What prize are *you* after? Is it worldly in nature or is it a heavenly crown?

Prayer

Dear heavenly Father, help me to keep my eyes on You. Keep me on the path You have planned for my life, and when I deviate from it, put me back on course.

Therefore submit to God. Resist the
devil and he will flee from you.
(James 4:7)

RESISTANCE

Resistance is defined as "refusal to give in to something." The most impactful example of resistance in my lifetime was the stand taken by Chinese men and women in Tiananmen Square. On April 15, 1989, student-led dissidents gathered to protest corruption within the Chinese Communist Party. Their list of demands included democratic reform and an end to both media censorship and restrictions on their freedom to assemble. As the number of protestors grew into the millions, the Chinese government instituted martial law. On June 3, Chinese tanks and soldiers opened fire on the protestors. What began as a peaceful demonstration turned into a bloody massacre. Not surprisingly, the western world only learned of the incident via smuggled video and photos. Among those images and video was a single man standing in front of a line of forward moving tanks. Whether "Tank Man" survived the mass execution is unknown, but his isolated bravery became a striking visual representation of resistance.

[Enter Jesus]

Matthew 3:13–17 documents Jesus' baptism by John the Baptist. When Jesus rose from the water, He saw the Spirit of God descending upon Him and a voice came from heaven saying, "This is my Beloved Son, in whom I am well pleased." The very next verse states: "Then Jesus was led up by the Spirit into the wilderness to be tempted by the devil" (Matthew 3:16–4:1). Note that the Holy Spirit *led* Jesus but it is not the one who *tempted* Him. If Jesus was led into temptation immediately following God's Spirit resting upon Him, it doesn't bode well for believers. It's as if God is forewarning us—once we believe in Him, watch out, because Satan will be coming for us, too.

James tells us to resist the devil, but how do we do that? After forty days and nights of fasting in the desert, Jesus was hungry. Typical of Satan, his first move was to go for the obvious weakness. He said, "If You are the Son of God, command that these stones become bread." But He answered and said: "It is written, 'Man shall not live by bread alone, but by every word that proceeds from the mouth of God'" (Matthew 4:3–4). From His own experience Jesus showed us how to resist temptation—submission to God and *scripture*. Jesus didn't resist temptation by reminding Satan Whom he was talking to; He resisted with God's word from Deuteronomy 8:3.

As if he were thinking, *two can play that game,* Satan then attempted to use the Word *of* God *against* God. He took Jesus to the highest point of the temple and said, "If You are the Son of God, throw Yourself down. For it is written: 'He shall give His angels charge over You' (Matthew 4:6) and, 'In their hands they shall bear You up, lest You dash Your foot against a stone'" (Psalm 91:11–12). Jesus responded again with scripture saying, "You shall not tempt the Lord your God" (Deuteronomy 6:16). But Satan was determined. He took Jesus atop a tall mountain overlooking all the kingdoms of the world and said, "All of these things I will give You if You will fall down and worship me" (Matthew 4:9). Finally, Jesus had enough and shouted, "Away with you, Satan! For it is written, 'You shall worship the Lord your God, and Him only you shall serve'" (Matthew 4:10; Exodus 20:3–5). Finally realizing Jesus could not be swayed, "the devil left Him" (Matthew 4:11).

If Satan was bold enough to tempt Jesus, he'll have no problem going after us. Thankfully, we have a Savior who experienced temptation and showed us how to be triumphant over it. Isaiah prophesied that the Messiah would be "a Man of sorrows and acquainted with grief" (Isaiah 53:3). Jesus experienced both suffering and temptation. He is our hope and our Redeemer. *He* is the One standing between us and the forces of evil. He helps us in times of trouble. Armed with God's Holy Word, we have the ammunition to fend off Satan and to be victorious in life.

Thoughts and Reflection

What are some problem areas in your life that cause you or your family to struggle? Ask the Holy Spirit to guide and help you identify scripture that is applicable to those situations and memorize it. Use the Word of God against Satan.

Prayer

Dear heavenly Father, thank You for giving me Your Word so that I can defend against the evil one. Thank You for Jesus, Who is intimately aware of what I experience every day.

Rejoice always, pray without ceasing, in everything give
thanks; for this is the will of God in Christ Jesus for you.
(1 Thessalonians 5:16–18)

T'ANKS FOR HELPING ME

*M*y granddaughter was very ill yesterday, and it's no wonder; like most toddlers, she licks everything within reach. Her most recent target was a toy ice cream cone she found at an indoor playground the day before. By the time I saw her tongue running over the germ-infested plastic, it was too late. The bacteria had been ingested and whatever was going to happen was going to happen—and it did, twenty-four hours later.

After seven documented episodes of vomiting, one episode of diarrhea, lots of gagging, and Mommy and Daddy washing and rewashing several loads of laundry, she was finally feeling better. Toward the end of her illness, she sat up and gagged one last time. As my daughter cradled her, holding back her long, blond hair, she looked up with a tiny smile and said, "T'anks for helping me."

[Enter Jesus]

As the virus worked its way through my granddaughter's system, there wasn't really anything her mother could do except let her know she was there loving her through it. Even though she was very sick, she felt safe and trusted her mother's love. Jesus longs to have this relationship with us. He longs for us to rest in Him, feel safe with Him, to "Trust in the Lord with all your heart, and lean not on your own understanding" (Proverbs 3:5).

I'm fairly certain why my granddaughter became ill, but many times the reason for personal struggles remains a mystery. We feel like we're drowning in life's difficulties, whether they're physical, financial, or spiritual. God wants us "in all" our ways, during the calm and the storm, to "acknowledge Him, and He shall direct" our paths (Proverbs 3:6).

Spending time trying to figure out why something happens, or trying to change what's happening, can be a waste of emotional resources. Yes, we need time to grieve and mentally process the situation, but ultimately God wants us to "Be anxious for nothing, but in everything by prayer and supplication, with thanksgiving, let your requests be made known to God; and the peace of God, which surpasses all understanding, will guard your hearts and minds through Christ Jesus" (Philippians 4:6–7).

In his music video for "Different," Micah Tyler recounts various family hardships: his grandmother's battle with cancer, home damage by Hurricane Harvey, and his younger brother's recent diagnosis of stage four cancer. His initial prayer had been, "Jesus, can You please just change these things?" But as time passed, he realized "sometimes the best question is not, Jesus can You change these things around me, but instead, God can You change *me* so that I can handle things that You're walking me through?"

Thanking God for difficult circumstances, rather than asking Him to *change* them, is Holy Spirit driven. Human nature typically prevents us from saying "thank you" after receiving a punch to the face. Human nature is to complain and punch back. However, in these moments of turmoil, could there be something God is trying to teach us—goodness, gentleness, patience, peace, love, joy, kindness, faithfulness, self-control, humility, dependence on Him, *thankfulness*?

The change that Jesus brings is a peace and thankfulness in *all* circumstances—not just the joyful moments, but the difficult ones as well. God wants to wrap His arms around us and comfort us, holding our hand as we weather life's storms. He promises, "For the

Lord your God, He is the one who goes with you. He will not leave you nor forsake you" (Deuteronomy 31:6). And, like an innocent child trusting in a mother's love, so sick and so tired, He wants us to look to Him in advance and say, "Thanks for helping me."

Thoughts and Reflection

Sometimes being thankful is reflexive, and at other times it must be intentional. Being thankful for a situation that brings you happiness is easy; being thankful for a situation that brings you grief is not. We can find comfort in knowing that God is in control; whatever happens, God is walking with us. Practice being deliberately thankful in all things and look for the lesson God is trying to teach.

Prayer

Dear heavenly Father, thank You for every aspect of my life. Help me to always see beauty in the lessons You have for me. Thank You for Your Holy Spirit, who is always with me. It's comforting to know "When you pass through the waters, I will be with you; and through the rivers, they shall not overflow you" (Isaiah 43:2)

Come, and let us return to the Lord; for He has torn, but He
will heal us; He has stricken, but He will bind us up.
(Hosea 6:1)

SOVEREIGN AND IN CONTROL

While watching a video last week I heard a Word of Faith pastor, Todd White, say, "Do you know how many people are mad at God because they've been taught that 'God's in control'? That's not even in the Bible. It's not. You won't find 'God's in control' in the Bible. It's not scripture." So, I went in search of, and found, several verses supporting the fact that God *is* in control of both good and bad, and that He *is* sovereign: Psalm 135:6, Psalm 115:3, 1 Samuel 2:6–8, and Romans 9:15–18. Proverbs 16:4 states: "The Lord has made all for Himself, yes, even the wicked for the day of doom." That's pretty solid language supporting God being sovereign and in control.

[Enter Jesus]

In Luke, the disciples were arguing about which one of them was the greatest. Jesus redirects the conversation to Peter by saying, "Simon, Simon! Indeed, Satan has asked for you, that he may sift you as wheat" (Luke 22:31). I don't know about Simon Peter, but I think I'd have said, "Please, Lord, tell me you told him *no*!" Jesus went on to say: "But I have prayed for you, that your faith should not fail" (Luke 22:32). Jesus didn't tell Satan, *no*—He instead prayed for Peter's faith. Peter bravely responds by telling Jesus that he's ready to go with Him even to death. Unfortunately, Jesus continued, telling him that before the rooster crowed, Peter would deny Him three times.

It would have been easy for Jesus to tell Satan "No," but would that have been best for Simon Peter? *Peter was hotheaded.* In the Garden of Gethsemane, he was the disciple who cut off the right ear of the high priest's servant (John 18:10). *Peter was impulsive.* After Jesus' resurrection the disciples were on a boat. John looked to shore and said, "It is the Lord!" Without hesitation *or* confirmation, Peter threw himself into the water and started swimming (John 21:7). And *Peter was a little sanctimonious.* In Matthew 26, Jesus tells his disciples that they would *all* fall away from Him, which would fulfill the prophecy in Zechariah 13:7: "Strike the Shepherd, and the sheep will be scattered." Not wanting to be lumped in with cowards, Peter replied, "Even if all are made to stumble because of You, I will never be made to stumble" (Matthew 26:33).

Even though Peter had a few negative, but very common, human characteristics, Jesus loved him. But He knew Peter needed to be polished, and therefore allowed him to be tested. Peter denied knowing Jesus or being one of His followers in a moment of great fear. The shame that followed fueled the disciple in the years to come. Never again would he deny his Lord and Savior.

Remember Job? By all accounts Job was a good man. He was *so* good he offered sacrifices to God for sins that his children *might* have committed (Job 1:5). Until recently I didn't understand why God allowed Job's suffering. Upon further study, Job's motive for living a good life came into question. Though he was righteous, was he living a good life to *honor* God, or was he living a good life in order to be *blessed* by God? Once tragedy struck, out of pride, Job challenged God's fairness. The Lord replied, "Where were you when I laid the foundations of the earth?" (Job 38:4). After being reprimanded, Job said, "Behold, I am vile; what shall I answer You? I lay my hand over my mouth" (Job 40:4).

God allowed Simon Peter to be tested by Satan to strengthen his faith and character, and God allowed Satan to take nearly everything from Job in order to refine Job's righteousness. The devil may walk to and fro looking for those he can devour, but there are limits to his power. Those limits are set by God. I may not understand *why*, but I find tremendous comfort in knowing that every circumstance of my life is determined by Him—for *His* purpose.

Thoughts and Reflection

Take a survey of your life and current hardships. Instead of submitting to the crashing waves of adversity, turn your eyes upward to Jesus and ask, "What are You trying to teach me?"

Prayer

Dear heavenly Father, help me. I'm overwhelmed and feel paralyzed. Show me what You want me to do. Make it obvious. Guide me through this maze of trouble, strengthen my faith, and refine my righteousness.

He who walks with wise men will be wise, but the
companion of fools will be destroyed.
(Proverbs 13:20)

GRAVITY

*I*t's easier to fall than it is to get back up, both literally and figuratively. Why? It's easier to fall *literally* because of gravity. Gravity is the "invisible force that pulls objects toward each other; Earth's gravity is what keeps you on the ground and what makes things fall," according to spaceplace.nasa.gov. It's easier to fall *figuratively* because of another invisible force—sinful human nature. Gravity, the invisible force, wins each and every time—unless a prevailing power intervenes.

We live in a close-knit neighborhood. *All* of the residents keep an eye on *all* of the kids. Like most parents, over the years we received phone calls from friends regarding a wide range of troubling behaviors from our children: our youngest not wearing a helmet while riding his bike, running across a busy road dodging cars, building forts on other people's wooded property, and our oldest driving too fast through the neighborhood. When our youngest was ten, there was a squabble within his little tribe. After watching friend "X" do something to another boy's bike, he gave friend "Y" an ultimatum—him or me. Unfortunately, Y chose X and our son was friendless for the entire summer—but he was OK with that.

Navigating friendships can be challenging at any age, but especially in the early years. Parents who draw lines in the sand over potentially harmful relationships can cramp the style of a youngster trying to enlarge their circle of friends. At one time or another most of us heard a parent say, "You are the people you surround yourself with," or "It's better to run alone than with a crowd running in the wrong direction." As it turns out, there's quite a bit of biblical support for those parental warnings.

[Enter Jesus]

You might be thinking, *Hold on a minute—didn't Jesus hang out with the wrong crowd?* Yes, He did. And when confronted by the Pharisees on this very fact He said, "Those who are well have no need of a physician, but those who are sick. I did not come to call the righteous, but sinners, to repentance" (Mark 2:17). Jesus was with the wrong crowd in order to redeem them, to call them "to repentance," not to socialize with them. Unlike the rest of us, He was the Son of God and was incapable of falling victim to sin— even when tempted by Satan himself. As born-again believers, we must always be watchful. Proverbs 4:23 states: "Keep your heart with all diligence, for out of it *spring* the issues of life."

Many times, a young person will befriend, date, or even marry someone in hopes of changing them. However, the apostle Paul warns against this: "Do not be unequally yoked together with unbelievers. For what fellowship has righteousness with lawlessness? And what communion has light with darkness?" (2 Corinthians 6:14). The reason for this caution is simple—gravity. It's easier to pull someone down than to lift them up.

We are all sinners and fall short of God's glory, but we need to exercise good judgment and choose wisely. As followers of Christ, there will be times when we will have to stand alone because we are a "new creation," and "the old things have passed away" (2 Corinthians 5:17). Inevitably, the "you think you're better than me" accusations will be hurled. But stand firm. It's not self-righteous to avoid situations, or people, that could potentially cause you to slide back into old ways; it is guarding your heart.

Though we are instructed to *love* others, it is not our job to *change* them. Conviction of sin and transformative change come through the Holy Spirit: "And when He has come, He will convict the world of sin, and of righteousness, and of judgment" (John 16:8). Our allegiance is to our heavenly Father. *He* is our audience—not our friends, social media acquaintances, or family. And, although gravity is a powerful force, Jesus is the *prevailing* power that will intervene as long as we continue walking in fellowship with Him.

Thoughts and Reflection

Are you struggling to maintain a godly lifestyle? Are you continuing to hold on to your old ways because you're afraid to step out of your comfort zone and make new friends?

Prayer

Dear heavenly Father, deliver me from anything in my life that does not bring honor to You. Protect me and my loved ones from anyone who has evil intentions. Give me courage to do what is right in Your eyes, even if it means breaking off friendships.

Jesus answered and said to him, "Most assuredly, I say to you, unless one is born again, he cannot see the kingdom of God."
(John 3:3)

WHAT YOU SEE IS WHAT YOU GET

"I can't change."
"It's part of my charm."
"I was born this way."
"It's just how I am."
"What you see is what you get."

Sound familiar? We use these excuses for anything and everything, but primarily for aspects of our personalities that are disagreeable—pride, stubbornness, arrogance, behaving sinfully, always having to be right, along with a hundred other reasons. Why? Maybe we think settling for the way we are is easier than trying to change. Maybe we like the edgy parts of our personalities and don't *want* to change. Maybe we're just rebels without a cause, charging into life's battles waving our flag of offensive behaviors and personality traits with pride.

During what was basically a one-sided discussion with my grandson, I said, "There are two of us in this conversation—why do you keep interrupting?" Without missing a beat he said, "That's just how God made me." Oh boy. If you're reading this, and you see yourself or a loved one in any of the above excuses, there's hope.

[Enter Jesus]

What you saw is what you got with Simon Peter. The disciple was a lovable mess, and I have always identified with him more than any of Jesus' other followers. He spoke before he thought (Mark 8:32–33), was bossy (Mark 9:5), loyal and impulsive (John

18:10), and weak of flesh (Matthew 26:36–46; Luke 22:55–62). If ever there was a flawed human being it was Peter, yet Jesus chose him—and it wasn't because of his charming personality. In any movie depiction of the disciples, Peter is almost always portrayed by a surly character, ready to fight at the drop of a hat. He was passionate, but also a bit erratic. When Jesus wanted to wash his feet, Peter said, "You shall never wash my feet!" Jesus answered him, "If I do not wash you, you have no part with Me" (John 13:8). Peter then replied in the extreme, telling Jesus to wash not only his feet, but his head and hands as well. And yet, regardless of his obvious love and devotion to Him, prior to Jesus' death, Peter denied Him three times. This guy was all over the place, even *after* he met Jesus. His flaws were obvious in the presence of the holy Son of God, and yet Jesus loved him—as He does each of us.

After witnessing Jesus' resurrection, however, a new Simon Peter emerged. The brazen "what you see is what you get" Peter was gone. Whatever shortcomings he was born with had faded. Peter *did* change. He changed because of having a personal relationship with Jesus, along with witnessing His resurrection. As we mature in our relationship with the Creator of all things, we will also change. Jesus is the Son of God and died for us while we were yet sinners. It is impossible for one to remain the same after encountering Jesus Christ on a personal level.

Does it mean we will be perfect, never make another mistake, and never sin? No. Even the new and improved Peter sinned. He was called out as a hypocrite over food laws by the apostle Paul: "Now when Peter had come to Antioch, I withstood him to his face, because he was to be blamed; or before certain men came from James, he would eat with the Gentiles; but when they came, he withdrew and separated himself, fearing those who were of the circumcision. And the rest of the Jews also played the hypocrite with him, so that even Barnabas was carried away with their hypocrisy" (Galatians 2:11–13).

Continuing to live a sinful life or engaging in behaviors that may harm us and our loved ones is not part of God's divine plan. No matter the sin, no matter how we think we were born, Jesus calls us to be *born again*. God loves us and wants us to come to Him just the way we are, but He loves us too much to leave us that way.

Thoughts and Reflection

Are you living a life that produces fruits of the Holy Spirit, or do you continue to struggle with behaviors that are displeasing to God? If you are still struggling after serious self-examination, do you truly *want* to change?

Prayer

Dear heavenly Father, help me to identify behaviors in my life that are not pleasing to You. Help me to *want* to change and help me to stop making excuses.

My knees are weak through fasting, and my
flesh is feeble from lack of fatness.
(Psalm 109:24)

FASTING

While searching for scripture related to fasting, I found the above verse in Psalm 109 and burst into laughter. I could barely see through the tears, and it took ten minutes to compose myself. This very morning my husband and I discussed getting a treadmill—and it isn't because either of us *lack* in fatness. My husband is very active, but after decades in the military and playing school sports he is no longer able to run like he used to. I am, in theory, *able* to run, I just don't enjoy it. I strictly adhere to, "The wicked run when no one is chasing them" (Proverbs 28:1 GNT). I am also heat intolerant, despise sweating, and don't like cold, windy weather. These aversions eliminate being outside at least three hundred days of the year in the Northeast. As far as fasting, I have admittedly never participated other than when I'm asleep—when my body is unable to access the pantry. Therefore, this topic is of genuine interest to me. Is it necessary for Christians to fast? When should one fast? And what's the real purpose in doing so?

By definition, fasting is to abstain from all or some kinds of food or drink for specific purposes. Intermittent fasting is currently a popular dieting trend, with many health benefits. It's not so much *what* you eat, but *when* you eat. "Essentially, fasting cleanses our body of toxins and forces cells into processes that are not usually stimulated when a steady stream of fuel from food is always present," according to the Boulder Medical Center. Personally, I prefer a steady stream of food, but let's explore the benefits of fasting from a *spiritual* standpoint.

[Enter Jesus]

In Matthew 6:17–18 Jesus said: "When you fast, anoint your head and wash your face, so that you do not appear to men to be fasting, but to your Father who is in the secret place; and your Father who sees in secret will reward you openly." Jesus said this in follow-up to calling out the Pharisees for distorting their faces and displaying "a sad countenance" so that everyone would *know* they were fasting (Matthew 6:16). Nevertheless, Jesus said *"when"* you fast, so, although there is no *command* to fast in the Bible, there must be benefits.

In Matthew 9:14–15 Jesus is asked by the disciples of John the Baptist: "Why do we and the Pharisees fast often, but Your disciples do not fast?" And Jesus said to them, "Can the friends of the bridegroom mourn as long as the bridegroom is with them? But the days will come when the bridegroom will be taken away from them, and then they will fast." The analogy Jesus used was a Jewish wedding feast, which was all about celebration, so it was ridiculous to consider fasting during that time. Since Jesus (the bridegroom) was present, the disciples did not need to fast—yet. The time would come, but not while Jesus was still with them.

Fasting is one way to focus our mind and body. Throughout the Old and New Testaments there were different purposes for fasting, which are still relevant today: to strengthen prayer (Ezra 8:23), seek the Lord's guidance (Judges 20:26–27), express grief (1 Samuel 31:13), seek God's help (2 Chronicles 20:3–4), show repentance (1 Samuel 7:6), overcome temptation (Matthew 4:1–11), and to express love and worship to God (Luke 2:37).

Additionally, fasting isn't just for food. In Philippians 4:8 the apostle Paul encourages us to keep our minds on heavenly things: "Finally, brethren, whatever things are true ... noble ... just ... pure ... lovely ... of good report, if there is any virtue and if there is anything praiseworthy—meditate on these things." One way to protect our mind is to fast from worldly distractions that confuse our priorities and prevent us from growing in faith: television, politics, sports, social media. Time is precious, and we are blessed with a finite amount—we should use it wisely. Ultimately, fasting is an individual choice. Whether you choose to participate or not, as the apostle Paul wrote in 1 Corinthians 10:31: "Whatever you do, do all to the glory of God."

Thoughts and Reflection

Have you ever fasted? If so, did you experience the intended spiritual benefits? If you've never fasted, ask God to direct you in this new experience.

Prayer

Dear heavenly Father, strengthen my resolve to become closer to You. Convict me of all aspects of my life where I need to either fast or completely abstain.

For there is nothing covered that will not be revealed, nor hidden that will not be known. Therefore whatever you have spoken in the dark will be heard in the light, and what you have spoken in the ear in inner rooms will be proclaimed on the housetops.
(Luke 12:2–3)

SECRETS, DECEPTION, AND LIES, OH MY!

*N*ational Treasure: Book of Secrets is one of my all-time favorite movies. Story line: Benjamin Franklin Gates, a treasure hunter-protector, embarks on a quest to prove his great-grandfather's innocence involving the Lincoln assassination. In pursuit of the truth, he holds the president of the United States hostage until he tells him the location of a ledger called the President's Book of Secrets. Once he and his team find the book, they realize it contains many revelations to long-held historical secrets like Area 51, the JFK assassination, and something the president himself wants to know about on page forty-seven.

Although a presidential book of secrets is fiction—probably—humans have been trying to keep things hidden since the beginning of time: Cain killing Abel, Franklin D. Roosevelt's paralytic condition, the Manhattan Project, every teenager—ever, and Colonel Sanders's original batter recipe, just to name a few. Not all secrets are bad, but if you've ever done anything wrong and have attempted to keep it hidden, you know how incredibly stressful it can be.

[Enter Jesus]

After Jesus ascended to heaven, Peter healed a lame man near the gate of the temple. He and John were arrested shortly thereafter for preaching Jesus' resurrection from the dead. Appearing before the Sanhedrin, Peter was asked by what power this miracle took place. He declared that it was through Jesus Christ that the man was healed. Unable to find a way to punish them, because the people were glorifying God for the man's healing, the religious rulers released them. The number of new believers was multiplying by the thousands, many of them selling their land and personal belongings. The proceeds from their possessions were then given to the disciples to disperse among other believers in need (Acts 3–4). Among the new converts were a man named Ananias and his wife Sapphira.

Ananias, with his wife's knowledge, had sold a piece of land but held back part of the money. It was their secret. On first glance it appears Ananias and Sapphira were just being sensible and did nothing wrong. However, Acts 5:4 records Peter confronting Ananias, saying: "Why have you conceived this thing in your heart? You have not lied to men but to God." Ananias didn't just withhold some money; he *lied* about withholding it. But the Holy Spirit knew and conveyed their secret to the disciple Peter.

The judgment for Ananias and Sapphira's deceit was swift. Immediately upon hearing Peter's accusation, Ananias "fell down and breathed his last" (Acts 5:5). Three hours later Sapphira came to Peter, and he confronted her as well. He asked if they had "sold the land for so much," and she said, "Yes, for so much." Whatever the amount, Peter, through the Holy Spirit, knew she was lying. He asked, "How is it that you have agreed together to test the Spirit of the Lord?" Sapphira immediately "fell down at his feet and breathed her last" (Acts 5:7–10). Obviously, intense fear fell upon everyone who heard what happened.

The realization that God knows everything we've ever done is a little scary. At some point in our lives we've all been guilty of trying to hide the truth, and hopefully we've asked forgiveness for those indiscretions. Not all secrets are bad (surprise gifts), and there are, in fact, some things God *does* want us to keep secret: something personal told to us in confidence (Proverbs 11:13), charitable deeds (Matthew 6:3–4), praying (Matthew 6:6), and fasting (Matthew 6:18). These actions done in secret honor our heavenly Father and demonstrate pure intentions and humility.

Whether it's cheating on our taxes, hiding things from our spouse, or anonymously giving to someone in need, God knows all that we've done and will "bring every work into judgment, including every secret thing, whether good or evil" (Ecclesiastes 12:14).

Thoughts and Reflection

Is there anything in your life where you need to come clean and get the truth out in the open? Lies and deceit will hold us captive, but John 8:32 tells us: "You shall know the truth, and the truth shall make you free."

Prayer

Dear heavenly Father, help me to always honor You by being truthful and avoiding situations that breed deceit. Keep my intentions pure in all that I do and guard my heart against secrets and lies.

*Finally, my brethren, be strong in the Lord and in the power
of His might. Put on the whole armor of God, that you
may be able to stand against the wiles of the devil.
(Ephesians 6:10–11)*

SUIT UP! (PART 1)

S uit up! This has been the most dreaded phrase in our house
for over twenty years and is, unfortunately, my husband's
all-time favorite. Along with these two words, as they echo
through the early morning hours, come visions of trimming bushes
and nut parties (picking up nuts buried in the grass). "Suit up"
means not only to get dressed, but to dress appropriately.

The apostle Paul was in Rome awaiting an audience with Emperor
Nero when he wrote his letter to the Ephesians. Ephesus was a
Roman province, the church there was in trouble, and Paul's
letter intended to address the problem—Jewish believers making
Gentile believers feel like lower-class citizens in God's kingdom.
The Ephesians needed to realize they were in a battle, but not one
of this world.

[Enter Jesus]

The apostle Paul had a literal come-to-Jesus moment on the road
to Damascus. Why him? Paul was unique. He was not only a Jewish
Pharisee well versed in Hebrew scripture, but also a Roman citizen.
This diverse background made Paul an effective witness for Jesus
Christ to the Gentiles.

In his letter, Paul is basically telling the Ephesians they have allowed
darkness to infiltrate their ranks. "For we do not wrestle against
flesh and blood, but against principalities, against powers, against
the rulers of the darkness of this age, against spiritual hosts of

wickedness in the heavenly places" (Ephesians 6:12). Since the Ephesians would understand Roman influences, Paul used the analogy of a Roman soldier's armor to illustrate what they would need to effectively combat these forces.

The first piece of armor listed by Paul is the *belt of truth*. "Stand therefore, having girded your waist with truth" (Ephesians 6:14). The belt was part of a Roman soldier's armor which held weapons; a dagger and sword. Paul uses the Greek word for truth, *aletheia*, in the context of *speaking* truthfulness in Ephesians 6:14, as well as Ephesians 4:13–15 and Ephesians 4:25. God's word is the truth. Jesus is "the way, the truth, and the life" (John 14:6). When we are not living lives girded or wrapped in truthfulness we become vulnerable to the enemy's influence. As Sir Walter Scott's saying goes, "Oh what a tangled web we weave, when at first we practice to deceive." A life of deception enables Satan to gain a foothold.

The second piece of armor crucial to defeating the enemy is also in Ephesians 6:14: "having put on the *breastplate of righteousness*." For the Roman soldier, the breastplate was a central piece of armor that protected the heart and other vital organs. Likewise, spiritually speaking, the breastplate of righteousness is meant to protect, or guard, our hearts. By ourselves we can never attain righteousness, and no amount of good works can get us there—we are made righteous through Jesus Christ. By obeying His commandments and living a life that honors Jesus, we guard our hearts against the enemy, against temptation, against false teachings, and against our own heart's wicked desires.

The third piece of armor is *"having shod your feet with the preparation of the gospel of peace"* (Ephesians 6:15). What made the Roman soldier's sandals unique was the sole. Similar to a pair of cleats, the sandals had gripping capability. Short, heavy-headed nails were used to reinforce the soles of the boot-like sandals, allowing the soldier to stand firm during battle. The gospel of peace, God's

Word, keeps us anchored, enabling us to stand firm when faced with the enemy's trappings.

As Christians we need to be grounded in the true gospel of Jesus Christ. As long as we are rooted in Him we are on stable ground and cannot be shaken. So get ready and suit up!

Thoughts and Reflection

As Christians, our most intense struggles are against the powers of darkness in this world, and once we realize this, it can be overwhelming. The existence of the unseen spiritual world around us can be intimidating, but Paul gives us instruction on how to defend against it—by putting on the whole armor of God.

Prayer

Dear heavenly Father, help me to prepare my armor; fix the belt of truth around my waist so that I will not be vulnerable to the evil one, clothe me in righteousness as I desire Your will and follow Your commandments, and plant my feet firmly in Your word, so that I can stand firm against the enemy.

Finally, my brethren, be strong in the Lord and in the power of His might. Put on the whole armor of God, that you may be able to stand against the wiles of the devil.
(Ephesians 6:10–11)

SUIT UP! (PART 2)

As a reminder, Paul was in Rome awaiting an audience with the emperor. The Jewish believers within the church in Ephesus were making Gentile believers feel like lower-class citizens, and Paul's letter was advising them to get a grip and realize the battle they were facing wasn't a battle of "them versus us" but was of a more serious nature—a battle against the rulers of darkness.

[Enter Jesus]

Paul initially persecuted the early Christian church—until he encountered the Savior on the road to Damascus. Like Paul's instruction to the troubled church in Ephesus, we need to be equally prepared to combat evil. Fortunately, we have been given a step-by-step method to do so.

The fourth piece of armor Paul writes about is the *shield of faith*: "above all, taking the shield of faith with which you will be able to quench all the fiery darts of the wicked one" (Ephesians 6:16). A Roman soldier's shield was made of thick animal hide. Before battle the soldier would dip his shield in water, so when the enemy's fiery darts hit the wet surface, the dampness would extinguish the flames. Satan's fiery darts come in the form of everyday things we're faced with: lustful temptations, fear, anxiety, hopelessness, greed, pride—the list is endless. We are bombarded from every direction by the forces of evil in this world. Our shield of defense is faith; faith is ground zero for a Christian's entire belief system.

Faith in God's truths prevents us from falling victim to the lies of the enemy. Faith is everything to a Christian; faith that God *is*, faith that Jesus has redeemed us, faith that all things will work together for our good, and faith in an eternal existence with Him beyond this life. Without faith we have no defense.

The fifth piece of armor is in Ephesians 6:17, which tells us to "take the *helmet of salvation*." Salvation comes the moment we put our trust in Jesus Christ. Recognizing we are sinners, repenting, trusting in His death as payment for our sins, and believing in His resurrection, we are made new and should live a life honoring our Lord and Savior. Like protective headgear used by soldiers today, the Roman soldier's helmet was crucial. A soldier can limp off the battlefield after incurring an array of injuries, but if the brain is affected survivability decreases. The mind is a battlefield like no other and is Satan's most effective target. When our mind is vulnerable to Satan, he causes us to feel doubt and discouragement. In 1 Thessalonians 5:8 Paul expands the helmet of salvation to include hope: "But let us who are of the day be sober, putting on the breastplate of faith and love, and as a helmet the hope of salvation." Our hope lies not in the securities of this world, but in the one to come, and if we allow Satan to interject doubt in the hope of our salvation, he wins.

The final piece of armor is the *"sword of the spirit*, which is the word of God" (Ephesians 6:17). A soldier's sword was used defensively as well as offensively; likewise, the word of God is both an offensive and defensive weapon. In 2 Timothy 3:16 Paul writes: "All Scripture is given by inspiration of God, and is profitable for doctrine, for reproof, for correction, for instruction in righteousness." We can trust what the Bible says to be from God, not just the whimsical writings of men. Hebrews 4:12 tell us: "For the word of God is living and powerful, and sharper than any two-edged sword … and is a discerner of the thoughts and intents of the heart."

God has given us a powerful weapon in the form of his Word. As we grow in maturity, hiding His Words in our heart, we can effectively defend against the evil one. We have heavenly armor and a mighty God behind us, so *suit up* and hold the line!

Thoughts and Reflection

Do you have an arsenal of weapons ready to defend against Satan? Have you memorized scripture, so when the need arises you are able to defend against him?

Prayer

Dear heavenly Father, thank You for the instruction You've given. Thank You for Your Word and the truth within its pages. Help me to be ready for battle at a moment's notice. Give me strength to withstand the enemy.

Brethren, if a man is overtaken in any trespass, you who are spiritual restore such a one in a spirit of gentleness, considering yourself lest you also be tempted.
(Galatians 6:1)

LOVING CORRECTION

We all know individuals who don't respond well to correction; they double down and dig in their heels when confronted. When this occurs, it can be frustrating; an employer refusing to acknowledge wrongdoing, a loved one's refusal to accept responsibility for their actions, a child's otherworldly stubbornness when attempting to teach them right from wrong, or someone resisting the corrective truth of the gospel.

Though it may be the *easier* thing to do, allowing someone to continue living in error is not an act of love—it is the *opposite* of love. Proverbs 3:12 states: "For whom the Lord loves, He corrects, just as a father the son in whom he delights." Correction comes in many forms. Whether it involves correcting behavior, correcting misinformation, or correcting inaccurate theology, telling someone the truth is the most loving thing you can do. Penn Jillette, of the magician duo Penn and Teller, once said, "How much do you have to hate somebody to not proselytize? How much do you have to hate somebody to believe everlasting life is possible and not tell them that?" Penn Jillette is an atheist.

[Enter Jesus]

Jesus addressed error and sin without hesitation, often confronting individuals publicly. His correction of the unbeliever, hypocrites, and those who opposed Him was harsher than for those who loved Him. In Matthew, Jesus was preaching to His disciples and the multitudes concerning the Pharisees and their hypocritical behavior. When speaking of the scribes and Pharisees, seven of the thirty-nine verses in Matthew 23 begin with "Woe to you." Jesus admonished the self-righteous leaders for being blind, fools, self-indulgent, and hypocrites. Then, in Matthew 23:33, He added the cherry on top, calling them "serpents" and a "brood of vipers." Outwardly, the Pharisees appeared to be the gold standard, but Jesus knew their hearts.

Most of Jesus' admonishments were verbal. However, in the Gospel of John He got physical. It was Passover and Jews from all over the region were descending upon Jerusalem for the holy feast. The temple, God's house, was being used for something *other* than worship: "And He found in the temple those who sold oxen and sheep and doves, and the money changers doing business. When He had made a whip of cords, He drove them all out of the temple … and poured out the changers' money and overturned the tables. And He said to those who sold doves, 'Take these things away! Do not make My Father's house a house of merchandise!'" (John 2:13–16). In this case, Jesus publicly corrected those who needed correction—with a whip.

Many people embrace the belief that God is love but reject the notion that God *hates* anything. The Bible, however, is clear—God hates sin: see Proverbs 6:16–19, Psalm 11:5, Revelation 2:6, Psalm 101:3, and Psalm 45:7. Although Jesus displayed mercy for the woman caught in adultery, refusing to condemn her along with those who wanted her stoned, He made His position clear—"Go and sin no more" (John 8:11).

Prior to Jesus' crucifixion, James and John asked to be placed on Jesus' right and left sides once He entered His kingdom. Jesus said, "You do not know what you ask. Are you able to drink the cup that I drink?" (Mark 10:38). His correction was to the point—*who do you two think you are?* There are many other examples of Jesus correcting His followers: see Matthew 8:23–27, Luke 10:41–42, Luke

13:1–5, John 21:21–22, and Mark 9:33–37. Jesus corrects those who love Him with compassion and patience. Like a parent correcting a child, His correction was, and will always be, done out of love. As Christians, we are not anyone's judge or jury. We are, however, commanded to spread the gospel and gently set a fellow believer right if they go astray, helping them back on the right path.

Thoughts and Reflection

Have you ever corrected someone and been met with opposition? Have you shared the truth of the gospel with someone and been met with rejection? If so, remember that *you* are not being rejected—the message is. Don't get discouraged; the negative response may be temporary. Don't underestimate the value of a lovingly planted seed.

Prayer

Dear heavenly Father, I want to live my life for You. When I am in error, correct me and get me back on track. Bring to light any sins against You or others, so that I can correct them.

But indeed for this purpose I have raised you up, that I may show My power in you, and that My name may be declared in all the earth. (Exodus 9:16)

MISSED OPPORTUNITIES

*I*n 1988, soon after I graduated nursing school, there was a week-long revival at my church. Pastor Richard Green was the guest pastor from South Africa. I was convicted during the first service about sharing the gospel—which, as an introvert, was terrifying to me. I worked the night shift on a medical-surgical unit in a city hospital, and that evening a young woman was admitted. Her name was Robin. She was disheveled in appearance, and looked as though she had lived a hard, sad life. I felt the nudge to speak to her about Jesus, but I was afraid—so I didn't. On night two the conviction was stronger, so on my way out of the sanctuary I picked up some gospel tracts lying on a table.

As I drove to work I prayed and asked God to make it obvious if I was supposed to share the gospel with Robin. I'm certain God laughed at that one—*of course* He wanted me to share the gospel with Robin. Nevertheless, that's what I prayed. I was already afraid, and there wasn't one thing about her that was approachable, so if God wanted me to share the gospel, He had His work cut out getting that conversation started. When I walked into her room on first rounds, I asked how she was doing. I don't remember her exact words, but as she stared out the window, she said something like, "I've been thinking about God lately." I nearly fainted. After recovering from the jolt of God answering my prayer *so* obviously, Robin and I began talking about Jesus. Before leaving the room, I asked if she would like more information about salvation. She said "yes," and I went to get the pamphlets. When I returned, she was in the bathroom, so I laid the tracts on her bedside table. She was asleep on every round thereafter. I should have prayed with her, but I didn't. She was discharged before my next shift, and I never saw her again. A couple of weeks later, on my day off, a woman called the hospital from an outside number and asked for me. She didn't leave her name, but I'll always wonder if it was Robin.

[Enter Jesus]

In a continuation of the Sermon on the Mount, Jesus tells the people: "But seek ye first the kingdom of God and His righteousness" (Matthew 6:33). He wants us to constantly seek Him and do His will. In everything we do we should have our minds set on Jesus. "Whatever you do in word or deed, do all in the name of the Lord Jesus, giving thanks to God the Father through Him" (Colossians 3:17). When we truly want Jesus to be in control of our life, He will gladly take charge and write our story. He is "the author and finisher of our faith" (Hebrews 12:2). God will provide us with many opportunities to share the plan of salvation with others, but we need to be ready—and willing.

Jesus gave the following command before He ascended to Heaven, and it is for *this* purpose we have been raised up: "Go therefore and make disciples of all the nations, baptizing them in the name of the Father and of the Son and of the Holy Spirit, teaching them to observe all things that I have commanded you" (Matthew 28:19–20).

Unfortunately, many of us are guilty of missed opportunities because of fear. We're afraid of being tongue-tied or getting negative reactions, verbal backlash, hate, and rejection. But Jesus said, "Do not worry about how or what you should answer, or what you should say. For the Holy Spirit will teach you in that very hour what you ought to say" (Luke 12:11–12). And, regardless of our fear, we are told to "always be ready to give a defense to everyone who asks you a reason for the hope that is in you" (1 Peter 3:15).

Thoughts and Reflection

Thinking back on your life, were there missed opportunities? If you had the chance to go back and change the situation, what would you do or say differently?

Prayer

Dear heavenly Father, forgive me for not listening to Your Holy Spirit when You nudge me to speak to someone about You and Your love for them. Give me the words I need to say when I need to say them. Let me honor You in all that I do.

Abstain from all appearance of evil.
(1 Thessalonians 5:22 KJV)

APPEARANCES AND ENTANGLEMENTS

S everal years ago, I read a popular novel and posted a rave review on social media. I received immediate backlash from some Christian friends and was shocked by their responses. I thought it was a great book, with a loving message, but their caution was sincere—be careful. A little insulted, I thought, *Do they really think I'm unable to discern incorrect theology from correct theology?* (Spoiler alert—I wasn't.) After some friendly back-and-forth, agreeing to disagree, we moved on, remaining friends. Years later, discussion of this same book and author resurfaced in a documentary I was watching. After further study, along with watching other interviews by the same author, I realized my friends were correct—and so was their public admonishment. By endorsing the book, it appeared I was also endorsing its heretical theology.

Years later I began reading another book, but then discovered the author had used psychography as a tool to write a different manuscript—jotting down words she *sensed* God was saying. So far, the book *I* was reading was without any obvious doctrinal red flags. But, concerned, I asked my husband what he thought. Without hesitation he said, "You already know what to do—avoid even the appearance of evil."

A familiar, public example of avoiding even the *appearance* of evil is former Vice President Mike Pence and his practice of never dining alone with a woman who isn't his wife. We all want to believe our reputations would be sufficient if an accusation of inappropriate behavior ever arose; unfortunately, sometimes the appearance of a thing is as powerful as the thing itself.

There is one way to avoid the appearance of wrongdoing: "Let us lay aside every weight, and the sin which doth so easily beset us" (Hebrews 12:1 KJV). According to Merriam-Webster.com, a besetting sin is "a main or constant problem," those sinful practices with which we continue to struggle.

[Enter Jesus]

We've all heard the phrase, "In it, not of it." Before His betrayal and crucifixion, Jesus prayed for His disciples: "I pray not that thou shouldest take them out of the world, but that thou shouldest keep them from evil. They are not of the world, even as I am not of the world. Sanctify them through thy truth: thy word is truth" (John 17:15–17 KJV). Knowing that His disciples could not help being *in* the world, Jesus' prayer was that they would not be *of* it, and that they would be kept from evil. Sometimes being kept from evil is an act of divine intervention, but more commonly it involves choice, avoiding situations that would cause one to stray from righteousness.

At times God will place us in situations and bring people into our lives for His purpose, but we should always be on guard. Ephesians 5:11 (KJV) states: "And have no fellowship with the unfruitful works of darkness, but rather reprove them." This verse deals with two separate issues: separating ourselves from works of darkness and reproving them (exposing them and calling them out). Unfortunately, when Christians separate themselves, choosing to avoid certain situations, they can be accused of being judgmental. The truth is, in these circumstances, a follower of Christ is simply adhering to the instruction of scripture. In John 7:24 (KJV) Jesus said: "Judge not according to the appearance, but judge righteous judgment." Jesus does not want us to judge a person superficially, only by what we see, but He does say to use "righteous judgment"— good judgment—discerning good from evil.

There are many biblical translations of 1 Thessalonians 5:22, the majority of which instruct the believer to avoid, reject, or abstain from all kinds of evil. The King James Version broadens the instruction of avoidance of evil to include even the *appearance* of it, and in the twenty-first century the latter translation is the more cautious one. While it's true that keeping up appearances can be a vain ambition, when our audience is Christ and our goals are appropriately focused on the eternal, appearances are crucial.

Thoughts and Reflection

Reflect on your daily routine—the movies and television shows you watch, the books you read, and the music you listen to. Do the subject matter, lyrics, and content honor God, or are they worldly, drawing you away from Him?

Prayer

Dear heavenly Father, I'm struggling with many things. I want to honor You, I want to do Your will, and I want to keep myself from all appearance of evil. Help me to eliminate the things that draw me away from You and Your will for my life.

You shall not take the name of the Lord your God in vain, for the
Lord will not hold him guiltless who takes His name in vain.
(Exodus 20:7)

WHAT'S IN A NAME?

A person's name is an extremely important aspect of their individuality, carrying cultural, spiritual, and historical significance. A name can provide a sense of belonging or separation, bringing happiness or sadness, depending upon parental wisdom. Parents name their children after all sorts of things: loved ones, fruit, stars, cars, compass directions, herbs—you name it and there's a child out there answering to it.

When your name comes up in conversation your ears, along with the rest of your body, turn in that direction—what did they say about you? Was your name used in the context of something complimentary, insulting, truthful, or was it false gossip?

In March 2020 my husband and I were fortunate enough to visit Israel, having no idea that in just a few days the whole world would change. On Friday, March 13, hotels began to close, holy sites shut down, and planes full of tourists at the Tel Aviv airport were being rerouted. Fortunately, our group was permitted to remain in Israel, but we lost our tour guide. One morning as we walked out of our hotel in Jerusalem, a group of women approached and handed us a pamphlet—a beautiful prayer for protection. Several sentences contained the word "G-d." I asked the reason for the hyphen and was told, "The word of God is so sacred that we don't write the entire name." What a contrast to the western world.

Merriam-Webster's online dictionary defines "vain" as having one of four meanings: 1) having or showing undue or excessive pride in one's appearance or achievements (conceited); 2) marked by futility or ineffectualness (unsuccessful, useless); 3) having no real value (idle, worthless); or 4) archaic (foolish, silly). In the context of Exodus 20:7, *vain* means "having no real value: idle, worthless." The phrase "take in vain" is defined as "to use (a name) profanely or without proper respect."

[Enter Jesus]

In Isaiah 42:8 the Lord speaks to Isaiah and says: "I am the Lord, that is My name; and My glory I will not give to another, nor My praise to carved images." The apostle Luke writes of Jesus in Acts 4:12: "Nor is there salvation in any other, for there is no other name under heaven given among men by which we must be saved." Paul writes in Philippians 2:10–11: "That at the name of Jesus every knee should bow, of those in heaven, and of those on earth, and of those under the earth, and that every tongue should confess that Jesus Christ is Lord, to the glory of God the Father." There is power in the name of the Lord God, Yahweh. There is power in the name of Jesus, Yeshua.

I frequently watch videos by Ray Comfort, a street preacher in California. He begins most conversations by asking people if they think they're a good person. Using the Ten Commandments as a guide he asks, "Have you ever told a lie? Have you ever stolen something? Have you ever substituted God's name for a curse word?" Nearly everyone answers "yes" to those three questions. He then asks, "Would you ever substitute your mother's name for a curse word?" Nearly 100 percent of the time the answer is "no." He then asks, "Why not?" The response? "Because I respect my mother."

Some will argue that "God" is not a name—it's a title. Therefore using "God" as a curse word isn't blasphemy. However, God's name and His title are inextricably linked. If someone threatens to harm the secretary of state, the Secret Service isn't going to care whether a proper name was used, because they know who the secretary of state is.

I believe the primary reason for using God's name loosely is that people just don't grasp the concept of true holiness. God is holy—and He is holier than we, as humans, can really fathom. So, whether blatantly cursing His name, typing a common three-letter acronym to express surprise, or shouting "Thus saith the Lord!" in order to manipulate a church congregation, using God's name without proper reverence is offensive to Him.

Thoughts and Reflection

Do you idly use God's name in everyday communication? In everything you do, ensure your words honor God.

Prayer

Dear heavenly Father, help me to treat Your name with the reverence and respect of which You are worthy. If I am doing or saying anything that dishonors You, bring it to my attention and help me to change.

Because he has set his love upon Me, therefore
I will deliver him; I will set him on high.
(Psalm 91:14)

STAY FOCUSED

*I*n 2013 a movie about the end of the world (as we know it) exploded onto the screen. *World War Z* revolves around a family: a man who had previously worked for the United Nations, his wife, and their two daughters. Individuals stricken with an unknown virus were infecting others in violent, animalistic fashion, biting and scratching. The film, like many disaster movies of its kind, highlighted the importance of being prepared for emergencies and having medications, food, and water on hand. The oldest daughter had asthma, and in the chaos of escaping Philadelphia all her emergency inhalers were left behind. After finding an abandoned RV the family heads for New Jersey. At one point the daughter experiences severe respiratory distress, and they have to pull the vehicle over. Her father gets down to her eye level and says, "Look at me. Look at me! Breathe in through your nose. We've done this a hundred times. *Look at me.*" The more the child focused on her father's reassuring voice and his instruction, the calmer she felt and the less labored her breathing became.

[Enter Jesus]

In Matthew 14 Jesus had just fed the five thousand (not including women and children) and was ready for a much-needed break. He told His disciples to get into a boat and go on ahead of Him, while He dispersed the crowd. Jesus then went alone to a mountainside to pray. While they were on the boat the wind picked up. Just before dawn Jesus came to them, walking on the water. Initially they were frightened, and then Peter cried out, "Lord, if it is You, command me to come to You on the water." So He said, "Come."

And when Peter had come down out of the boat, he walked on the water to go to Jesus." All was well—until Peter's focus drifted from Jesus to the storm around him. It was at that moment, when he lost focus, that Peter began to sink, crying out, "Lord, save me!" And immediately, Jesus stretched out His hand and caught him, and said to him, "O you of little faith, why did you doubt?" (Matthew 14:28–31).

Most of us probably identify with Simon Peter more than any other disciple. He loved Jesus with his whole heart, yet continued to doubt; he followed Jesus, but continued to question; he worshipped Jesus, but continued being impulsive and, at times, a little self-righteous. Like Peter, we all have days when it feels like we're surrounded by crashing waves. Jesus wants us to keep our eyes on Him, to focus on the One who can grab hold of our hand, lift us up out of the waves, and calm the turbulent winds.

Through Jesus Christ, God the Father has given us direct access to Him. He provides relief from turmoil, and like He did with Peter, immediate rescue—if we stay focused. Isaiah 26:3 promises: "You will keep him in perfect peace, whose mind is stayed on You, because he trusts in You." This verse illustrates that *perfect peace* begins and ends with God; we are nestled in between, those whose minds are *stayed on* and who *trust* in Him. This doesn't mean we won't suffer devastating losses or live a worry-free life. What it does mean is that God will provide us with an indescribable sense of peace within those tumultuous moments.

Perfect peace is otherworldly. It is not a feeling of happiness or an ignorant bliss that all is well. It is the calm within the storm, freedom from the guilt of past sin, the indescribable joy amid sorrow. It is "the peace of God, which surpasses all understanding" (Philippians 4:7).

At any moment our world can be turned upside down and all that we know and trust can be shattered. But, even in the midst of tragedy, we can have the perfect peace of Isaiah 26:3 if we stay focused on Jesus. Philippians 4:6 tells us: "Be anxious for nothing, but in everything, by prayer and supplication, with thanksgiving, let your requests be made known to God." *This* is when we will experience His peace that passes all understanding.

Thoughts and Reflection

Do you ever experience inexplicable peace in the midst of chaos, or do you tend to focus on the storm around you? What can you do to more fully experience the peace of God?

Prayer

Dear heavenly Father, keep me focused so that I can experience Your "perfect peace" no matter what is going on around me.

And you, fathers, do not provoke your children to wrath, but
bring them up in the training and admonition of the Lord.
(Ephesians 6:4)

A GOOD FATHER

The meaning of "do not provoke your children to wrath" is pretty straightforward—don't antagonize your children to anger. Interestingly, Paul directs this command to fathers, not mothers. Why? In *general*, it's more natural for a woman to be nurturing and for a man to be aggressive, to push, to be task-oriented, focusing less on a child's emotional needs and more on achievement.

Though it's possible for children raised by single parents to thrive, there are two startling statistics to consider regarding absent fathers. According to the Texas Department of Corrections, "85% of youths in prison grew up in fatherless homes." The U.S. Department of Justice reports that "63% of youth suicides involve a child who was living in a fatherless home when they made their final decision." Children need both male and female influences in their lives—*godly* male and female influences.

[Enter Jesus]

In John 3:16 Jesus says: "For God so loved the world, that He gave His only begotten Son, that whoever believes in Him should not perish, but have everlasting life." God loves His children so much that He sent Jesus, who willingly died so that we might have eternal life. Fathers (and mothers) should strive for this type of sacrificial relationship with their children, putting the child's needs ahead of their own.

For those who did not have a godly father as a role model, trusting in a loving heavenly Father can be challenging. Children of alcoholic fathers may experience a pleasant man one minute and an abusive man two hours later. Constantly walking on eggshells, never knowing which side of a personality you will encounter, produces anxiety and insecurity. Our heavenly Father, however, does *not* change (Malachi 3:6), and there will never be a time when you will wonder what you're going to get with God. "The Lord is gracious and full of compassion, slow to anger and great in mercy" (Psalm 145:8).

In families where children experience the injustice of favoritism, at times a result of their own parent's insecurities, feelings of worthlessness can abound. One sibling seems to do no wrong, while another never quite measures up, resulting in hurtful phrases like, "Why can't you be more like your brother or sister?" But, with God, "all His ways are justice, a God of truth and without injustice; righteous and upright is He" (Deuteronomy 32:4). He created each one of us differently for *His* purpose. We are all unique; so unique, in fact, that in a world of nearly eight billion people, not one of us has the same fingerprint. We were "fearfully and wonderfully made" (Psalm 139:14), with beautiful, distinct characteristics, and God loves each one of us equally.

Unfortunately, an ungodly father may also have unrealistic expectations for his children. When a child inevitably falls short there can be terrible consequences—physical and psychological. He may push them harder physically to improve in sports or push them to study longer hours to improve their academic standing. Perfection is expected, without a reasonable way to achieve it— again, producing anxiety. God is different. He meets us where we are, flaws and all. Jesus loved and died for us while we were sinners (Romans 5:8), and when we decide to follow Him our old self will pass away (2 Corinthians 5:17). We will never be perfect, but Christ was perfect *for* us. Jesus died on the cross so that through Him we have a way to the Father.

Fathers play such a critical role in representing God to their children. All a man's God-given, innate characteristics, when coupled with love and submission to his *own* heavenly Father, will result in a godly parent. God's love is perfect. He will never antagonize, belittle, or ask something from us without providing a way to achieve it. And when we stray, when we repent, He will be there with forgiving, open, loving arms, welcoming us back to Him.

Thoughts and Reflection

If you were not raised by godly parents, the only way to free yourself from the bondage of resentment is to forgive. After all, your bitterness is hurting *you* more than it's hurting *them*. If you believe you've failed as a parent, it is never too late to submit yourself to your heavenly Father and ask for His healing.

Prayer

Dear heavenly Father, help me to become the person You want me to be. If I am harboring anger, bitterness, and resentment toward my own parents, please forgive me and release me from that burden.

THE LORD IS MY SHEPHERD

Psalm 23 is one of the most treasured passages in scripture. Our world is filled with turmoil, not unlike the era in which King David lived. David was riddled with flaws, and yet to God he was "a man after His own heart" (1 Samuel 13:14). Written by a shepherd turned King, from the perspective of one *needing* a shepherd, Psalm 23 paints a striking depiction of who God is and who He wants to be for His children.

[Enter Jesus]

Jesus is the Good Shepherd and gave His life for His sheep (John 10:11). *"The Lord is my shepherd"* (Psalm 23:1) is descriptive of the relationship God wants to have with us. He wants to be our compass, leading us through life's stormy trials.

"I shall not want" (Psalm 23:1) describes provision. As children of a loving God, He will supply us with all our needs.

"He makes me to lie down in green pastures" (Psalm 23:2) is a description of safety and rest. The shepherd creates a safe place for his sheep to lie down; likewise, God provides safety and rest for His children under His ever-watchful eye.

"He leads me beside the still waters" (Psalm 23:2). The Hebrew words for *still waters* are *Mai Menochot*, meaning *restful waters*—in contrast to turbulent and dangerous waters. Jesus is described as the source of living water and is the life-giving water for our souls.

"He restores my soul" (Psalm 23:3) means exactly that—restoration. Like wandering sheep, all of humanity is prone to stray. When we

lose our way, we can be assured the Good Shepherd will redirect us, restoring our joy and fellowship.

"He leads me in the paths of righteousness" (Psalm 23:3) describes guidance. The path of righteousness may not be the safest or swiftest route, but it provides the believer with the opportunity to trust the Shepherd's leadership.

"For His name's sake" (Psalm 23:3) indicates purpose. Everything in a believer's life should be for the purpose and glory of their heavenly Father.

"Yea, though I walk through the valley of the shadow of death, I will fear no evil, for You are with me" (Psalm 23:4) indicates the darkness of tribulations we face in life. Though this passage is often read at funerals, darkness (rather than death) is more befitting the context of a shepherd protecting his flock. We face darkness in various forms every day, but we don't need to fear during these moments because we have the protection and faithfulness of the Almighty; "the One who goes with you," promising He will "not leave you nor forsake you" (Deuteronomy 31:6).

"Your rod and Your staff, they comfort me" (Psalm 23:4). The shepherd uses his rod and staff to defend sheep against predators, keep them on the right path, pull them from entanglements, and lift them up after falling. Likewise, our heavenly Father shields, saves, and directs His children.

"You prepare a table before me in the presence of my enemies" (Psalm 23:5) illustrates provision and victory over enemies—a victory so complete that our heavenly Father will set the celebratory table Himself.

"You anoint my head with oil" (Psalm 23:5) has significance for both literal sheep and for followers of Christ. A shepherd rubs oil on his sheep's nose to prevent the larvae of flies from hatching and

burrowing into the soft flesh of the sheep's nasal passages. Without this preventive measure, inflammation and infection could cause a sheep to harm itself while attempting to relieve the pain. Anointing one's head with oil was a sign of being set apart, being blessed by the Lord. Priests were anointed with oil, and 1 Peter 2:9 states that believers "are a chosen generation, a royal priesthood."

"My cup runs over" (Psalm 23:5) illustrates abundant provision. God will supply the believer with more than is expected; a life overflowing with His presence and protection, as well as an abundance of spiritual blessings.

"Surely goodness and mercy shall follow me all the days of my life" (Psalm 23:6) indicates that, though we are undeserving, God will pursue us with His goodness and mercy.

"And I will dwell in the house of the Lord forever" (Psalm 23:6) is a beautiful statement of eternal security. When the day comes for the believer to pass from this life into the next, they will have everlasting life in the presence of the Lord, in a place Jesus has prepared for us (John 14:3).

Prayer

Dear heavenly Father, thank You for the loving promises of Psalm 23, Your protection, Your blessings, and for the day when I will dwell with You forever.

Look at the birds of the air, for they neither sow nor reap nor gather into barns; yet your heavenly Father feeds them. Are you not of more value than they?
(Matthew 6:26)

VALUABLE

For nearly ten years I worked alongside the most amazing group of people, with diverse personalities and backgrounds. Some had lived through traumatic experiences that should have destroyed them but instead left them with the loving heart of a servant. Some appeared hard and callous outwardly, yet they melted in the presence of a hurting child. Some were gentle in spirit and sought to make peace at every turn. Some were externally sweet and bubbly, but underneath beat the fierce and loyal heart of a protective lioness. Some were calm, cool, and collected on the surface, but struggling and broken underneath. And some were out-of-this-world *extra*. Though we were all very different, a common purpose unified us—caring for children. None of these individuals have notoriety or fame, but they are precious and valuable—because *God* loves them.

Unfortunately, too many people believe value is determined by success, wealth, beauty, intelligence, or good deeds. If value was determined by success or wealth, Elon Musk would be the most valuable person alive, with a net worth of over $200 billion dollars. If beauty was the determining factor—it's a toss-up; there are just too many physically attractive people out there. If value was determined by intelligence, Terence Tao would probably get the vote, with an IQ of 230; although I'm sure Stephen Hawking would disagree. If good deeds were the deciding factor, the prize would probably go to twenty-three-year-old Jimmy Donaldson, aka Mr. Beast, whom my son told me about just last night. Donaldson is a famous YouTuber, with ninety-one million subscribers. He is

YouTube's leading charity donor. He lives in an ordinary-sized house and doesn't really care about money—unless he's giving it away. In evaluating all of the above, the one thing they have in common is that each of the determining factors of value is fleeting; wealth can be lost in a day, intelligence can vanish with one tragic head injury, beauty fades, and good deeds are subjective and transient.

[Enter Jesus]

As followers of Christ, our value doesn't lie in *who* we are, but in *Whose* we are. God doesn't love us because we are valuable; we are valuable because He loves us. As believers, when we question who we are, failing to realize that we have been chosen by God before the foundation of the world (Ephesians 1:4), it is impossible to make wise decisions. When we are not firmly grounded in our identity as sons and daughters of the King, not realizing that we have been made in the image of God (Genesis 1:26), we can be easily swayed by the enemy. When we don't comprehend what our adoption into God's kingdom cost Him (John 3:16), we can't possibly understand how truly loved we are.

In order to grasp how valuable we are, we first need to realize God rejoices over us (Zephaniah 3:17), that Jesus wants us to know His Love so that we can experience the fullness of God (Ephesians 3:19), and that God wants to bless us with more than we can even think to ask of Him (Ephesians 3:20).

Once we're ready to accept that we are valued by the Creator, and that through Jesus' sacrifice we have been made worthy, we need to "walk worthy of the calling" (Ephesians 4:1):"bearing with one another in love" (Ephesians 4:2); "endeavoring to keep the unity of the Spirit in the bond of peace" (Ephesians 4:3); and putting aside our former behavior to "be renewed in the spirit of your mind" (Ephesians 4:22-23).

Todd White, a popular Word of Faith pastor, once said: "The cross to me isn't the revelation of my sin, the cross is actually the revealing of my value." This is false teaching. The cross doesn't reveal our value, the cross reveals our wickedness—it wasn't our *value* that nailed Jesus to the cross, it was our *sin*. Even though sinful, human nature is why Jesus needed to shed His blood, "God demonstrates His own love toward us, in that while we were still sinners, Christ died for us" (Romans 5:8).

Thoughts and Reflection

Are there past behaviors in your life that make it difficult for you to accept that you are valued and loved by God? No matter what you've done, God loves you (1 John 4:10).

Prayer

Dear heavenly Father, help me to accept that I am valuable, not because of anything I've done but because of what You've done for me.

*Arise, go to Nineveh, that great city, and cry out against
it; for their wickedness has come up before Me.
(Jonah 1:2)*

JONAH

*I*f you were to ask my grandson his favorite Bible story, Jonah
and the whale would definitely be in the top three. After all,
being swallowed by a great fish and living to tell the tale
is pretty spectacular. Unfortunately, for many people the most
memorable part of Jonah's story is being swallowed and then
vomited onto dry land. However, there is a much deeper message
of mercy, love, and justice that we, as Christians, can glean from
the prophet's story.

[Enter Jesus]

Jesus Himself referenced Jonah, comparing the three days and
nights He would spend in "the heart of the earth" after His death, to
Jonah being in the belly of the great fish for three days and nights
(Matthew 12:40). There are other similarities between Jonah and
Jesus, but what I would like to explore are the similarities between
Jonah and *us*.

Jonah's story begins with God telling him to go to the city of
Nineveh and warn the people they were going to be destroyed
because of their wickedness. Jonah was a prophet, and at that
moment, he didn't like what he was hearing. Instead of following
God's instruction, Jonah ran away. This is difficult for many of us
to believe—God *audibly* spoke to him, gave him an assignment,
and Jonah refused. God wasn't asking him to sacrifice his life; He
was asking him to deliver a message. It doesn't seem that hard.
At some point after boarding a boat to Tarshish, which happened
to be sailing in the *opposite* direction of Nineveh, a terrible storm

developed. The fearful sailors asked Jonah who he was, and he replied, "I am a Hebrew; and I fear the Lord, the God of heaven, who made the sea and the dry land" (Jonah 1:9). Again, hard to believe that a prophet deliberately disobeys God, but says he fears the Lord. Nevertheless, because he knew he was the cause of the storm, Jonah told the sailors to toss him into the turbulent waters.

After being swallowed by the great fish that God had prepared, Jonah had three days to reflect on his attitude and actions. Jonah 2 documents his seemingly repentant prayer, and God, being merciful, caused the fish to vomit Jonah onto dry land—land, coincidentally, that happened to be only a day's walk to the gates of Nineveh (Jonah 3:4). Finally deciding to follow God's instruction, Jonah announced to the city of 120,000 that within forty days Nineveh would be overthrown. Jonah 3:5–10 reveals the people, from the king to the least citizen, repented and turned from their wicked ways, fasting and putting on sackcloth. As a result of their genuine repentance, God spared Nineveh—and this enraged Jonah. He was so upset that he wanted to die. He told God that he *knew* the Lord would be merciful and slow to anger, and that's why he fled to Tarshish in the first place (Jonah 4:2–3). Jonah would rather have seen 120,000 souls destroyed than saved. Once again, unbelievable—or is it?

Jonah didn't like the fact that God wanted to redeem Nineveh, so he ran away. He said he feared God, yet blatantly disobeyed Him. To Jonah, the people of Nineveh were the *worst*. Nineveh was the capital of Assyria. They were ruthless enemies of Israel, and Jonah wanted his own sense of justice carried out. How often do *we* want our own sense of justice pronounced upon those who have hurt us or someone we love? Do we pray for God to *redeem* them, or do we pray for God to *punish* them? God doesn't audibly speak to most of us, but we have His Word—how often do we deliberately ignore biblical instruction?

As Jonah acknowledged, He is "a gracious and merciful God" (Jonah 4:2). Humanity should be thankful for His mercy, because if God decided to purge the world of *all* evil, just the tiniest sliver of self-examination would result in an "uh-oh" moment for every single one of us. Our desire for immediate justice, our imperfect sense of justice, would surely come back to haunt us.

Thoughts and Reflection

Do you see yourself in Jonah? Do you say you fear God, and then deliberately disobey Him? Is there someone you've been led to witness to, but you hesitate—because you think they're the *worst*?

Prayer

Dear heavenly Father, forgive me for my disobedience and wanting my imperfect justice over Your perfect justice. Help me to love my enemies and pray for those who persecute me.

Lying lips are an abomination to the Lord, but
those who deal truthfully are His delight.
(Proverbs 12:22)

PANTS ON FIRE

The 1997 movie *Liar Liar* is about a lawyer, Fletcher Reede, who has a history of lying—to everyone. Fletcher's lies and broken promises were affecting his son so badly that on his birthday he wished for his dad to stop lying for just one day. The physical comedy that followed, as Fletcher struggled with telling the truth, was hysterical. It was impossible not to laugh out loud as the lawyer, unable to lie, struggled to represent his obviously guilty clients in the courtroom.

According to Science of People, "The average person lies once to twice per day." Personally, I think those are pretty conservative numbers. I recently took inventory of my own storytelling and discovered that I lie a lot more than I thought I did. For instance, when my husband asks how I'm feeling, I usually say "fine," whether I feel fine or not. After all, if I feel bad why should he? There was also a period when I had to take my blood pressure daily. One morning he asked me about the results, and I deliberately lied because I didn't want him to worry.

There are degrees of lies, from white lies to whoppers, and the world has been rocked by some pretty big ones: The tobacco industry claimed cigarette smoking was not harmful; Milli Vanilli admitted to never having sung on their albums or in concerts; Bill Clinton gave false testimony about having an inappropriate relationship with an intern; and Brian Williams, who claimed to have been in a helicopter that was shot down by RPG fire in Iraq. Since the beginning of time, humans have been lying for one reason or another.

[Enter Jesus]

Matthew 19 records Jesus counseling a rich, young ruler. The man asks, "Good Teacher, what good thing shall I do that I may have eternal life?" (Matthew 19:16). Jesus tells him if he wants to have eternal life, he needs to keep the commandments. The man then asks, "Which ones?" Jesus said, 'You shall not murder,' 'You shall not commit adultery,' 'You shall not steal,' 'You shall not bear false witness,' Honor your father and your mother,' and 'You shall love your neighbor as yourself'" (Matthew 19:18–19). Basically, all of them. Jesus reaffirmed the Ten Commandments to the man, and among them is don't lie—don't bear false witness.

In a 2010 article from *Everyday Health*, "The Truth About Telling Lies," Deirdre Lee Fitzgerald, PhD, states: "Research has linked telling lies to an increased risk of cancer, increased risk of obesity, anxiety, depression, addiction, gambling, poor work satisfaction, and poor relationships." Not only does lying offend God, it's bad for our physical and emotional health.

The focus verse states that lying is an "abomination," defined by Merriam-Webster as "something regarded with disgust or hatred." That's quite a condemnation of something most of us are guilty of doing every day. Nevertheless, lying and deceitfulness are sins. Peter writes of Jesus that He "committed no sin, nor was deceit found in His mouth" (1 Peter 2:22). The apostle Paul wrote in Colossians 3:9–10: "Do not lie to one another, since you have put off the old man with his deeds, and have put on the new man who is renewed in knowledge according to the image of Him who created him." We are created in the image of God and of Jesus (Genesis 1:26), and our behavior should reflect Christ.

Lying is a habit, one not easily broken. The first step in correcting any behavior is acknowledging the problem. Next, ask yourself the following question: Why do I lie? Is it to be more interesting, to get out of trouble, to keep from hurting another's feelings or making them worry, or some other reason? Then, consciously commit to always telling the truth. Before speaking, *think*—if it isn't true, don't say it. As followers of Jesus our lives should mirror Him, not Satan—who is "a liar and the father of it" (John 8:44).

Thoughts and Reflection

How hard is it to only allow *truth* to proceed out of our mouths? Take an inventory of situations in which you tend to lie. Pause and choose to only speak words of truth. It boils down to this—does telling a lie, even a white lie, honor God?

Prayer

Dear heavenly Father, as King Solomon wrote in Proverbs 30:8: "Remove falsehood and lies far from me." Convict me of any lies that leave my lips, forgive me for them, and help me to only speak words of truth.

*Let no corrupt word proceed out of your mouth, but what is good
for necessary edification, that it may impart grace to the hearers.
(Ephesians 4:29)*

WORDS

*O*ur six-year-old grandson loves telling jokes; unfortunately, very few of them ever make sense. He recently went through a phase of joke telling to his great-grandmothers on FaceTime, using ill-mannered words related to various bodily fluids and functions. Though his Papaw could relate to the childish humor, we had to have a talk with him about using inappropriate language, especially when conversing with his elders. Having overcome the use of impolite speech (for the most part), he decided to debut his newest joke Saturday night:

Him: "Mamaw, I have a joke—and the word 'poop' is *not* in it."
Me: "Fantastic. Fire away."
Him: "Why did the number ten cross the road?"
Me: "Because number nine told him to?"
Him: "No! To get to an alphabet concert! Isn't that hilarious?!"
Me: "Buddy, you're getting a joke book for Easter."

[Enter Jesus]

In Matthew 15 the Pharisees are at it again, this time complaining about the disciples' lack of hand washing. Jesus turned the tables and decided to educate them on what *truly* defiles a person. In Matthew 15:18–19 Jesus said: "But those things which proceed out of the mouth come from the heart, and they defile a man. For out of the heart proceed evil thoughts, murders, adulteries, fornications, thefts, false witness, blasphemies."

In 2017, a Massachusetts woman was found guilty of involuntary manslaughter after she told her "friend" to get back into his truck, the cab of which was filled with lethal fumes. The woman listened as he died, without trying to help. After the ruling, a *New York Times* article quoted the concern expressed by an ACLU lawyer, who stated, "This is saying that … her words literally killed him, that the murder weapon here was her words. That is a drastic expansion of criminal law in Massachusetts." Our words are powerful; they have the ability to build up or tear down, to bless or to curse. "Death and life are in the power of the tongue" (Proverbs 18:21).

Whether we are speaking to our friends, children, spouses, coworkers, neighbors, or posting on social media, the words we choose are important. The jokes we tell, and the language within them, are important. Our words reflect our character. As Christians, our words reflect Jesus—they aren't "just words." James 3:10 states: "Out of the same mouth proceed blessing and cursing. My brethren, these things ought not to be so."

I don't know who decided which words qualified as curse words, but the fact is, in today's society there is a generally accepted list of expressions that are considered objectionable. If you would like to view the directory, go to noswearing.com/dictionary. I assure you, there is a complete list from A–Z for your viewing displeasure. Regardless of whether you or I find a word objectionable, someone else might, and the use of it could cause them to ask, "If Christians speak the same as everyone else, what makes them different?"

Many times, in the heat of a volatile argument, our words can be vicious. In an effort to win said argument, we plunge in the verbal knife and give it a twist. But Proverbs 15:1 states: "A soft answer turns away wrath, but a harsh word stirs up anger." Exercising verbal self-control can diffuse an argument that would otherwise explode into a volcano of words that cannot be taken back—or forgotten.

King David displayed great wisdom when he penned the following in Psalm 141:3: "Set a guard, O Lord, over my mouth, keep watch over the door of my lips!" Whether it's a comment, joke, words said in anger, or an opinion of which the entire world must be made aware, use your words wisely. Remember, "Whoever guards his mouth and tongue keeps his soul from troubles" (Proverbs 21:23).

Thoughts and Reflection

Our words are powerful. Go to openbible.info/topics and in the search bar type "our speech." You will see one hundred verses regarding "our speech" within the Old and New Testaments. Proverbs 6:16–19 lists the six things that the Lord hates, three of which are related to our speech: "a lying tongue," "a false witness," and "one who sows discord." If this is an area where you struggle, like me, make this a prayer focus.

Prayer

Dear heavenly Father, I am painfully aware of the power of my words. Convict me of moments when I use them in opposition to Your will. Help me to always represent You well, speaking words of life to others.

Behold, the Lord's hand is not shortened, that it cannot save;
nor His ear heavy, that it cannot hear. But your iniquities
have separated you from your God; and your sins have
hidden His face from you, so that He will not hear.
(Isaiah 59:1–2)

FEELING SEPARATED

*A*s believers, we've probably all had moments when we *felt* separated from God. The closeness we once had seems to be gone. The fellowship we once had seems to have dissolved. Even our own desire to be near Him has faded. The question is—why?

[Enter Jesus]

Jesus experienced separation from God on the cross. The moment the sins of the world, mine and yours, were placed upon Him, He experienced the agony of separation from His heavenly Father. At that moment, when our iniquities were placed upon Him, God hid His face from His Son—for a moment.

Although there is controversy surrounding this subject, according to Isaiah 59:1–2, *sin* causes separation from God and causes Him to hide His face from us. Jesus never sinned. He was God in the flesh and incapable of sin. However, God's hatred of sin was felt by Jesus, and in that moment, He said, "My God, My God, why have You forsaken Me?" (Mark 15:34; Psalm 22:1). According to *The Putting Green Devotional* by Sam Hunter, "His cry of "My God, my God, why have you forsaken me?" … is simply a Remez (a hint), alerting his followers to all the promises we see in the Psalm." The last few verses of Psalm 22 *are* full of promises, but if Hunter is correct, Jesus' words of despair, uttered as He hung on the cross, would be disingenuous.

So, was Jesus separated from God in that moment? I believe He was. Did God reject or stop loving Him? No. Additionally, at no moment did Jesus cease being the holy, sinless Son of God. Though Jesus did experience separation from intimate fellowship with His heavenly Father when our sins were laid upon Him, He did not experience rejection or loss of love. The apostle Paul writes in Romans 8:38–39: "For I am persuaded that neither death nor life, nor angels nor principalities nor powers, nor things present nor things to come, nor height nor depth, nor any other created thing, shall be able to separate us from the love of God which is in Christ Jesus our Lord." Nothing can separate us from God's love, but because we are human we will continue to sin, and sin causes God to hide His face from us—that feeling of separation. Fortunately, the Holy Spirit convicts and prompts us to seek God's forgiveness, restoring our relationship with our heavenly Father.

Human feelings are unreliable. Basing your faith on *feelings* you have at any given moment is dangerous—and Satan knows we are prone to this. He would like nothing better than to make a believer *feel* separated from God, causing doubt. This is why 1 Peter 5:8 tells us: "Be sober, be vigilant; because your adversary the devil walks about like a roaring lion."

Emotions change and moods shift, but God never changes. "Every good gift and every perfect gift is from above, and comes down from the Father of lights, with whom there is no variation or shadow of turning" (James 1:17). Jesus and His words will never change. "Jesus Christ is the same yesterday, today, and forever" (Hebrews 13:8).

When we have *feelings* of hopelessness, like God has forsaken us, or we *feel* separated from Him, remember these words: "Fear not, for I am with you; be not dismayed, for I am your God. I will strengthen you, yes, I will help you, I will uphold you with My righteous right hand" (Isaiah 41:10). And when *feelings* begin to overshadow faith, remember, "For whatever is born of God overcomes the world. And this is the victory that has overcome the world—our faith" (1 John 5:4). It's our faith, not *feelings*.

Thoughts and Reflection

Do you *feel* separated from the Father? Is there something in your life, a current sinful practice, which could be the cause? If not, remember that confusion and hopelessness are not from God. Paul writes in 1 Corinthians 14:33: "God is not the author of confusion, but of peace." And Jeremiah 29:11 states that for those who love Him, God has "thoughts of peace and not of evil, to give you a future and a hope."

Prayer

Dear heavenly Father, remove all sin from my life. If I am unaware of a sinful practice, bring it to light. Help me rely on Your promises, not my *feelings*.

But the fruit of the Spirit is love, joy, peace, longsuffering,
kindness, goodness, faithfulness, gentleness, self-control.
(Galatians 5:22–23)

BY THEIR FRUITS

We all know a person who just seems filled with goodness and peace 24-7, no matter their circumstances. A person who has been on the receiving end of terrible injustice and tragedy, yet somehow manages to walk through life with a smile on their face and love in their heart—someone who seems too good to be true, who simply exudes joy. I know such a person. Her gentleness and kindness are authentic. When she asks how you're doing she isn't just being polite—she really wants to hear about it. I also know, without a doubt, if I called her right now crying my eyes out, she would be on my doorstep within minutes. And honestly, we're more acquaintances than friends—she's just that sweet. She's a woman of faith, and it shows.

[Enter Jesus]

In Matthew 7 Jesus is continuing the Sermon on the Mount and is speaking to the people concerning false prophets. In Matthew 7:16-20 He says: "You will know them by their fruits. Do men gather grapes from thorn bushes or figs from thistles? Even so, every good tree bears good fruit, but a bad tree bears bad fruit. A good tree cannot bear bad fruit, nor can a bad tree bear good fruit. Every tree that does not bear good fruit is cut down and thrown into the fire. Therefore by their fruits you will know them." These verses distinguish a believer from a nonbeliever. One is filled with the Holy Spirit and bears "good fruit." One is not and bears "bad fruit."

In Galatians, prior to writing about the fruit of the Spirit, the apostle Paul defines the "bad fruit" spoken of by Jesus as "works of the flesh." Works of the flesh include "adultery, fornication, uncleanness, lewdness, idolatry, sorcery, hatred, contentions, jealousies, outbursts of wrath, selfish ambitions, dissensions, heresies, envy, murders, drunkenness, revelries, and the like; of which I tell you beforehand, just as I also told you in time past, that those who practice such things will not inherit the kingdom of God" (Galatians 5:19–21).

The good fruit spoken of by Jesus, the "fruit of the Spirit" as described by Paul, is in opposition to fleshly works and desires. These qualities do not come naturally, and are manifested when one's life has been changed by Christ—showing *love* in the face of hate, *joy* amid sorrow, *peace* in the presence of chaos, *long-suffering* (enduring something unpleasant, with patience), *kindness* in the face of cruelty, *goodness* in the face of wickedness, *faithfulness* in the face of disloyalty, *gentleness* in the face of brutality, and *self-control* in the face of temptation.

As we grow spiritually, desiring God's will above our own, the Holy Spirit changes us. By spending time in His word and prayerfully seeking His guidance, we will become more like someone we never thought we could be—more like Jesus. On our own this is impossible, "but with God all things are possible" (Matthew 19:26).

There's no shortcut to changing your life. Anyone who has been through a twelve-step program will tell you that real change requires a lot of committment: admitting powerlessness, finding hope in a power greater than yourself, surrendering, taking moral inventory, admitting to yourself and God your wrongdoing, asking God to remove your shortcomings, making amends, praying and meditating, and helping others. Though there are certainly cases where individuals have had a miraculous, sudden change of heart and lifestyle, conversions like this are more uncommon than not. Few things worth having are acquired easily, and yet there is one goal that cannot be attained by human effort alone—a change of heart. By allowing God's word to renew our minds and transform the way we see ourselves and those around us, our hearts will become more like Jesus.

We will continue to struggle and continue to sin—that's why we need Jesus. What we cannot do on our own, we can do through Him. We're fallible and weak of flesh, but His "strength is made perfect in weakness" (2 Corinthians 12:9).

Thoughts and Reflection

Many of us struggle with the fruits of the Spirit—I *really* struggle with self-control. A life overflowing with *all* of the fruits of the Spirit seems humanly unattainable—and it is—that's the point. We cannot achieve all these attributes without Jesus.

Prayer

Dear heavenly Father, I pray that Your Holy Spirit, who dwells within me, will change me. Help me to display the fruit of Your Holy Spirit daily and be a light to others.

Trust in Him at all times, you people; pour out your
heart before Him; God is a refuge for us.
(Psalm 62:8)

I MESSED UP

I read something on social media several days ago that really hit home. The origin of the post appears to have been a tweet by Pastor Gavin Ortland. His intent was to contrast religion with the Gospel:

Religion: "I messed up. Dad's gonna kill me."
The Gospel: "I messed up. I need to call Dad."

Someone who messed up a *lot* was a man after God's own heart, King David. He coveted his neighbor's wife, stole the man's wife, and then had the man killed (2 Samuel 11). Possibly as a result of his miserable failings, coupled with God's forgiveness, King David wrote some of the most beautiful passages in the Bible. In his older, wiser years, having already committed many indiscretions, David wrote: "The steps of a good man are ordered by the Lord, and He delights in his way. Though he fall, he shall not be utterly cast down; for the Lord upholds him with His hand" (Psalm 37:23–24). Although King David committed many sins, he knew that genuine repentance resulted in forgiveness, as well as the restoration of relationship with his heavenly Father.

Unfortunately, many religions and denominations focus more on fear, guilt, and shame than they do on love and forgiveness. While it's true that we have all messed up (Romans 3:23), and there has only been one truly *good* person ever to have lived (Mark 10:18, 1 Peter 2:22), through that one person God provided a way to salvation.

[Enter Jesus]

Because humans will always mess up and will always sin, a sacrifice was needed to redeem us. John 3:16 states: "For God so loved the world that He gave His only begotten Son, that whoever believes in Him should not perish but have everlasting life." Jesus was that sacrifice. We need only "confess our sins," and when we do, "He is faithful and just to forgive us our sins, and to cleanse us from all unrighteousness" (1 John 1:9).

For those who feel unworthy of salvation, Jesus also spoke of the Father's pursuit of the lost. "If a man has a hundred sheep, and one of them goes astray, does he not leave the ninety-nine and go to the mountains to seek the one that is straying? And if he should find it, assuredly, I say to you, he rejoices more over that sheep than over the ninety-nine that did not go astray. Even so it is not the will of your Father who is in heaven that one of these little ones should perish" (Matthew 18:12–14).

Bearing in mind that although we are all his creation (Genesis 1:26), not everyone is a child of God (Matthew 7:21). Once we decide to live for Jesus and not ourselves (Romans 14:7-8), we are adopted into God's family and are heirs with Jesus Christ (Romans 8:17). 1 John 3:1 states: "Behold what manner of love the Father has bestowed on us, that we should be called children of God!" We are His children—and God is good to His children. Jesus said in Matthew 7:9–11: "Or what man is there among you who, if his son asks for bread, will give him a stone? Or if he asks for a fish, will he give him a serpent? If you then, being evil, know how to give good gifts to your children, how much more will your Father who is in heaven give good things to those who ask Him!" God loves us—each and every one of us.

Unfortunately, because we are human, we will continue to sin and make mistakes (1 John 1:8). However, the Holy Spirit will convict us of that sin (John 16:7-8), and when we confess our sin God will forgive us (1 John 1:9). Though a true follower of Christ cannot continue living a life of sin (1 John 3:6), when we go astray we have an advocate with the Father (1 John 2:1).

Satan accuses the brethren before God day and night (Revelation 12:10). He is a liar (John 8:44), whose purpose is to kill, steal and destroy (John 10:10). Although Satan cannot steal our salvation (John 10:27-30), he can certainly steal our joy. When you are living for Jesus, yet experience shame from past sins that return to haunt you, call your Father. God is not waiting to condemn; He is *a refuge for us*. As King David wrote, though we may fall, we *shall not be utterly cast down*.

Thoughts and Reflection

If you have chosen to follow Jesus and are truly living for Him, are there areas of your life where you have asked forgiveness but still feel condemned? If so, remember: "There is therefore now no condemnation to those who are in Christ Jesus, who do not walk according to the flesh, but according to the Spirit" (Romans 8:1).

Prayer

Dear heavenly Father, I am thankful that I can put my trust in Your Word. Thank You for Your sacrifice, mercy, and forgiving me when I stray off course.

When the Lord began to speak by Hosea, the Lord said to Hosea:
"Go, take yourself a wife of harlotry and children of harlotry, for the
land has committed great harlotry by departing from the Lord."
(Hosea 1:2)

ASTOUNDING LOVE

The 2022 film *Redeeming Love* is a modern-day twist on the story of Hosea (not recommended for children due to mature content, partial nudity, and violence). The main character, Michael Hosea, is a farmer during the 1850s California Gold Rush. While praying for God to protect his farm he adds, "Lord, I was hoping that maybe you might provide me with someone I can share this with. Maybe she likes fishing. You know, maybe she has long legs. Anyway, you know the kind I need. I trust you." Fast forward—Michael goes into town and sees Angel, who is a prostitute. Michael is made aware of this, but he doesn't care. God doesn't exactly tell him Angel is the one he prayed for, but Michael knows this is the woman God has led him to. The movie is, at times, painful to watch. Angel has suffered terrible abuses in her life, and though Michael continues his loving pursuit of her, she has no context for that kind of love and has difficulty accepting it. Sadly, far too many people can identify with Angel's inner struggle—I'm not worthy, and I don't deserve or understand true, unconditional love.

God's prophets didn't exactly have it easy. They were ridiculed, threatened, persecuted, and of the sixteen major and minor Old Testament prophets, six of them were martyred. But what God asked of Hosea was arguably the most challenging. Not only might he suffer all of the above. God told him to marry a harlot and remain faithful to her no matter what. Why? What good could possibly come from an ordained prophet of God subjecting himself to the pain and humiliation of marital infidelity?

[Enter Jesus]

The *old* covenant with Israel took the form of a marriage covenant at Mount Sinai after the Israelites were led out of bondage in Egypt. After receiving the Ten Commandments, "Moses took the blood, sprinkled it on the people, and said, 'This is the blood of the covenant which the Lord has made with you according to all these words'" (Exodus 24:8). At the Last Supper, Jesus "took the cup after supper, saying, 'This cup is the new covenant in My blood, which is shed for you'" (Luke 22:20).

The analogy of God's relationship with His people in the context of marriage is illustrated several times throughout the Old and New Testaments. In Isaiah 54:5 God refers to Himself as Israel's "husband"; in Jeremiah 3:14 the Lord tells Israel, "I am married to you." In Matthew 9:15 and John 3:29 Jesus refers to Himself as the "Bridegroom," and in Revelation 19:7 John writes: "Let us be glad and rejoice and give Him glory, for the marriage of the Lamb has come, and His wife has made herself ready."

Hosea was called to be a living representation of God's love for His people. At that time the nation of Israel was divided into the northern kingdom of Israel and the southern kingdom of Judah. Hosea was a prophet from the northern kingdom. He was well aware of Israel's sins. The people were breaking God's laws and had fallen into idol worship; in essence, Israel was committing spiritual adultery. God commanded Hosea to take a wife whom He *knew* would break their vows, and in spite of Gomer's adultery Hosea was to love her—mirroring God's unfailing love for a people He knew would continue breaking their vow with Him.

Despite our persistent unfaithfulness to our heavenly Father, He remains faithful to us. Gomer continued violating her marriage vows and she eventually fell into slavery. Hosea, who had every right to give up on her, redeemed her for a price and brought her home. God had every right to give up on Israel, and on us, yet He "demonstrates His own love toward us, in that while we were still sinners, Christ died for us" (Romans 5:8).

Thoughts and Reflection

Being purchased from slavery by her prophet husband must have been mortifying for Gomer. At the lowest point in her life, she was shown an astounding love that she neither understood nor deserved. God doesn't care who you were before Him. Jesus bought you with His blood, and you are now His beloved.

Prayer

Dear heavenly Father, thank You for Your astounding love. Help me to forgive myself, as You have already forgiven me. Thank You for making me worthy through the precious blood of Jesus.

BLESSINGS

The Greek translation of "blessed" also means "happy." Society encourages us to seek happiness within the temporary things of life; relationships, success, fun. God, however, desires that we seek happiness in Him. "Happy are the people whose God is the Lord!" (Psalm 144:15). The Sermon on the Mount begins with a series of eight blessings designed to prepare Christ's followers for His kingdom: a series of truths in drastic opposition to the world.

[Enter Jesus]

Matthew 5:1–2 states: "And seeing the multitudes, He [Jesus] went up on a mountain, and when He was seated His disciples came to Him. Then He opened His mouth and taught them, saying:

"Blessed are the poor in spirit, for theirs is the kingdom of heaven" (Matthew 5:3). The poor in spirit are those who realize they desperately need God and are nothing without Him. This humility will result in the inheritance of God's kingdom.

"Blessed are those who mourn, for they shall be comforted" (Matthew 5:4). Building upon the first beatitude, *those who mourn* means those who are genuinely sorrowful for their sin. Sorrowful repentance will result in comfort and restoration of relationship with God.

"Blessed are the meek, for they shall inherit the earth" (Matthew 5:5). Meekness is not weakness; it is power restrained. It is an attitude of humility, a strong but gentle spirit of unselfish commitment to God and submission to His will.

"*Blessed are those who hunger and thirst for righteousness, for they shall be filled*" (Matthew 5:6). The words hunger and thirst indicate desperation—a desperate desire for righteousness and to do the will of God. If we truly yearn for God's will above all else, we will be filled; He will satisfy our hunger and quench our thirst.

"*Blessed are the merciful, for they shall obtain mercy*" (Matthew 5:7). This strikes at the heart of those who hold onto grudges and are quick to condemn. If we expect God to be merciful to us, we are required to show mercy to others. Hosea 6:6, which Jesus references in Matthew 9:13 and Matthew 12:7, states: "For I desire mercy and not sacrifice, and the knowledge of God more than burnt offerings." Mercy can seem unfair—until you need it yourself.

"*Blessed are the pure in heart, for they shall see God*" (Matthew 5:8). This beatitude speaks to those with pure intentions. God knows everything about us; *what* we do and *why* we do it. He wants our actions to be humble, not self-seeking. Jesus said in Matthew 6:3: "When you do a charitable deed, do not let your left hand know what your right hand is doing." If one of your own hands shouldn't know what the other is doing, neither should anyone else.

"*Blessed are the peacemakers, for they shall be called sons of God*" (Matthew 5:9). In John 14:27 Jesus says: "Peace I leave with you, My peace I give to you; not as the world gives do I give to you." Every believer should seek to live in peace with others (Hebrews 12:14), and be grounded in the gospel of peace, as Paul wrote in Ephesians 6:15. We should strive to be peacemakers; spreading the good news that true peace is possible with God.

"*Blessed are those who are persecuted for righteousness' sake, for theirs is the kingdom of heaven*" (Matthew 5:10). This is a blessing filled with promise for those who suffer for doing what is right. When we're persecuted for doing something bad, we deserve it. There's no honor in it. But when people "say all kinds of evil against you falsely for My sake" (Matthew 5:11), we should rejoice and be glad, for our reward will be great in heaven. To rejoice is to have inner joy, which is present even amid sorrow and pain.

Followers of Christ are to be the salt of the earth and a light to others. We should recognize our desperate need for God and be sorrowful for sin, humble, show mercy, crave righteousness, be pure of intention, be peacemakers, and feel blessed when we are persecuted for righteousness's sake—of such is the kingdom of heaven. As long as we seek first the kingdom and His righteousness, God will provide all our needs (Matthew 6:33).

Thoughts and Reflection

As you read the beatitudes, are there some you struggle with more than others? Do you find humility, meekness, or the thought of being happy about being persecuted for the sake of righteousness challenging?

Prayer

Dear heavenly Father, help me to want what You want for my life. Help me to be humble, repentant, and desire Your righteousness above my own.

Who Himself bore our sins in His own body on the
tree, that we, having died to sins, might live for
righteousness—by whose stripes you were healed.
(1 Peter 2:24)

PSA

J have been a Christian for many years, but until recently never realized there was a theological term assigned to the belief that Jesus had to die on the cross for our sins—Penal Substitutionary Atonement (PSA). Although a core tenet of the Christian faith, PSA has some major opponents. Those in opposition to Penal Substitutionary Atonement question why Jesus had to die, why God can't just forgive us, and how Jesus' death made it possible for us to go to heaven.

According to theopedia.com, Penal Substitutionary Atonement is defined as "the doctrine that Christ died on the cross as a substitute for sinners. God imputed the guilt of our sins to Christ, and He, in our place, bore the punishment that we deserve. This was a full payment for sins, which satisfied both the wrath and the righteousness of God, so that He could forgive sinners without compromising His own holy standard."

Groups that reject PSA include churches that preach a watered-down gospel, who focus primarily on God's love and avoid preaching against, or using the term, "sin." Another group, postmodernism, believes everything is relative, and there are no absolute truths. And the Emerging Church movement embraces postmodernism and believes that as culture changes, so should the church.

[Enter Jesus]

In Mark 10:45 Jesus said: "The Son of Man did not come to be served, but to serve, and to give His life a ransom for many." But why did Jesus *have* to die? Why was the shedding of His blood necessary? Since the beginning of time blood has been sacrificially shed (Genesis 4:4). In the Old Testament, sin offerings were offered outside the camp (Leviticus 4:12; Leviticus 6:11; Leviticus 16:27; Exodus 29:14), and those sacrificial animals had to be perfect—flawless, without blemish or defect (Numbers 29:29; Leviticus 3:1; Ezekiel 46:13). Blood sacrifices outside the camp were a foreshadowing of the crucifixion of Christ, who "also, that He might sanctify the people with His own blood, suffered outside the gate" (Hebrews 13:11–12). The author of Hebrews also clearly answers the question by writing: "And according to the law almost all things are purified with blood, and without shedding of blood there is no remission" (Hebrews 9:22).

The answer to why God can't just forgive us lies in the characteristics, or attributes, of God. God is *infinite* (1 Timothy 6:16), *never changes* (Malachi 3:6), *self-sufficient* (John 5:26), *omnipotent* (Revelation 1:8), *omniscient* (Isaiah 46:9–10), *omnipresent* (Psalm 139:7–10), *wise* (Romans 11:33), *faithful* (2 Timothy 2:13), *good* (Psalm 34:8), *just* (Deuteronomy 32:4), *gracious and merciful* (Psalm 145:8), *love* (1 John 4:7–8), and *holy* (Revelation 4:8). God's love and justice go hand in hand. A judge who would release a murderer, without penalty, would neither be just nor loving to the family of the victim, or to possible future victims. Punishment for sin is required.

Every day, human beings cry out against injustice. We are outraged when someone is wronged and punishment isn't immediate and harsh. How much greater should our Creator's outrage be against sin? His sense of justice is perfect, ours is flawed. God *will* "just forgive us"—when we ask. But, like the unrepentant child who refuses to say, "I'm sorry, I won't do it again," all who are unrepentant will be held accountable.

Jesus' death made it possible for us to go to heaven because He *willingly* took our sins upon Himself (John 10:18; 1 Timothy 2:6; 1 John 3:16; John 10:11; John 10:15; Galatians 2:20). Though there are some who believe Penal Substitutionary Atonement equates to divine or cosmic child abuse, this belief is an insult to the Savior. Jesus wasn't a reluctant child dragged kicking and screaming to the cross—He came to earth specifically for that purpose, so that we might have eternal life through Him (John 3:16). Daniel Hames expressed it best: "It's no use pitting 'vindictive God' against 'innocent Jesus,' for the one nailed to the tree is Himself the sin-hating, sinner-saving God. The Son's complicity in His own condemnation as our substitute is one of the gospel's most glorious truths."

Thoughts and Reflection

The reality that someone would willingly die in place of another is difficult to grasp. That Jesus died to save you and me, before we realized we needed or even *wanted* saving, is an act of love difficult to comprehend.

Prayer

Dear heavenly Father, thank You for Your Son, Jesus. Thank You for His willing sacrifice for me, an undeserving sinner.

*The head of every man is Christ, the head of woman
is man, and the head of Christ is God.
(1 Corinthians 11:3)*

*Husbands, love your wives, just as Christ also
loved the church and gave Himself for her.
(Ephesians 5:25)*

*Wives, likewise, be submissive to your own husbands,
that even if some do not obey the word, they, without a
word, may be won by the conduct of their wives.
(1 Peter 3:1)*

HUSBANDS AND WIVES

The role of women within the home and society is a subject of great debate, and nothing makes a woman bristle like telling her she needs to be submissive. We all have our *opinions* on the matter, but more importantly, God has *instruction* on the matter. Considering the touchy topic, now is the perfect time for Jesus to take center stage, so ...

[Enter Jesus]

Jesus was unlike any other first-century man. In an age when women were viewed as second-class citizens, Jesus valued women and had women followers. A notable example of Jesus' high regard for women was His relationship with Mary Magdalene, who was delivered from the possession of seven demons (Luke 8:2). She was at the cross when He died (John 19:25), provided financial support to His ministry (Luke 8:2–3), and was the first person He appeared to after His resurrection (Mark 16:9).

Jesus spoke to women openly, which defied first century practice. He spoke to the Samaritan woman at the well (John 4:27), the woman caught in adultery (John 8:10–11), the woman with a twelve-year bleeding disorder (Mark 5:34), and many others (Luke 11:27–28; Luke 13:12; Luke 23:27–31).

It wasn't simply that Jesus spoke to women publicly; it was *how* He spoke to them. He called them "daughters" and "daughters of Abraham," making them of equal standing in God's kingdom (Mark 5:34; Luke 13:16). God created *both* male and female (Matthew 19:4); one is not more valued than the other. Supporting biblical equality of men and women within the body of Christ, the apostle Paul wrote in Galatians 3:28: "There is neither Jew nor Greek, there is neither slave nor free, there is neither male nor female; for you are all one in Christ Jesus."

Order prevents chaos—even animals have a social hierarchy. Likewise, within a marriage, God has ordained an established order. Man was created first (1 Timothy 2:13), and because it was not good for him to be alone, God created woman to be the man's helpmate (Genesis 2:18). This does not mean a woman should not be an equal decision-making partner within a marriage. This is why woman was created—to work alongside and help her husband.

Look again at the focus verses from Ephesians and 1 Peter. Who has the more difficult task? In ideal circumstances the man's responsibility is far more difficult—to love sacrificially, as Christ loves. If a man loves his wife as Christ loves the church, it will be easier for her to be submissive to his authority. However, godly marriages depend upon both a man and a woman. If a husband's behavior is not Christlike, a wife's submission will be difficult. Likewise, if a wife's behavior is contentious, it will be difficult for her husband to love as Christ loves.

Thoughts and Reflection

Submission to authority is challenging for many people, some more than others. Do you struggle with being submissive, either to God or your spouse? If so, why?

Prayer

Dear heavenly Father, make my marriage one that is pleasing to You, and help my actions toward my spouse honor You.

Special Note

Although a spouse's godly conduct may lead their partner to Christ, 1 Peter 3:1 must be read within the framework of the entire Bible, God's authority, and Jesus' teachings on love, mercy, and forgiveness. In relationships where domestic violence is present, professional and legal intervention is necessary. If both spouses are Christians, legal and professional intervention, coupled with spiritual counseling, would be appropriate.

God does not endorse abuse, nor does He excuse it (Luke 12:45–46). It's true that Malachi 2:16 states: "The Lord God of Israel says that He hates divorce." And Jesus said in Matthew 19:9: "Whoever divorces his wife, except for sexual immorality, and marries another, commits adultery; and whoever marries her who is divorced commits adultery." However, Psalm 11:5 states of God: "The wicked and the one who loves violence His soul hates." In Matthew 12:11–12 Jesus said to the Pharisees: "What man is there among you who has one sheep, and if it falls into a pit on the Sabbath, will not lay hold of it and lift it out? Of how much more value then is a man than a sheep?" Of how much more value, then, is the life of the abused? Jesus said, "I desire mercy and not sacrifice" (Matthew 9:13; Matthew 12:7). To expect anyone, or their children, to remain in a dangerous situation is not merciful. Ultimately, these difficult decisions are between the individual and God. And, like Jesus, the church body should demonstrate love and mercy.

Therefore God also has highly exalted Him and given Him the name which is above every name, that at the name of Jesus every knee should bow, of those in heaven, and of those on earth, and of those under the earth, and that every tongue should confess that Jesus Christ is Lord, to the glory of God the Father.
(Philippians 2:9–11)

PROPHECIES FULFILLED

*D*epending upon the source, there are estimated to be between three hundred and four hundred Old Testament prophecies related to the Messiah. In 1963, Peter Stoner, chairman of the Departments of Mathematics and Astronomy at Pasadena College, along with six hundred students, looked at eight specific prophecies about Jesus. Their conclusion: "The prospect that anyone would satisfy those eight prophecies was just 1 in 10^{17}"—in other words, a one in one hundred quadrillion chance. Stoner described it like this: "Suppose that we take 10^{17} silver dollars and lay them on the face of Texas. They will cover all of the state two feet deep. Now mark one of these silver dollars and stir the whole mass thoroughly, all over the state. Blindfold a man and tell him that he can travel as far as he wishes, but he must pick up one silver dollar and say that is the right one. What chance would he have of getting the right one? Just the same chance that the prophets would have had of writing these eight prophecies and having them all come true in any one man, from their day to the present time, providing they wrote using their own wisdom" (*Science Speaks: An Evaluation of Certain Christian Evidences*).

This one in one hundred quadrillion chance is based upon a single person fulfilling eight messianic prophecies; we will review ten.

[Enter Jesus]

Prophecy 1: The Messiah will be born in Bethlehem (Micah 5:2).
Fulfilled: "Now after Jesus was born in Bethlehem of Judea in the days of Herod the king" (Matthew 2:1).

Prophecy 2: The Messiah will be born of a virgin (Isaiah 7:14).
Fulfilled: "Now in the sixth month the angel Gabriel was sent by God to a city of Galilee named Nazareth, to a virgin betrothed to a man whose name was Joseph, of the house of David. The virgin's name was Mary… Then the angel said to her, 'Do not be afraid, Mary, for you have found favor with God. And behold, you will conceive in your womb and bring forth a Son, and shall call His name Jesus'" (Luke 1:26–31).

Prophecy 3: The Messiah will be preceded by a messenger (Malachi 3:1).
Fulfilled: Jesus said of John the Baptist: "For this is he of whom it is written: 'Behold, I send My messenger before Your face, Who will prepare Your way before You'" (Matthew 11:1–10).

Prophecy 4: The Messiah would enter Jerusalem on a donkey (Zechariah 9:9).
Fulfilled: "They brought the donkey and the colt, laid their clothes on them, and set Him on them" (Matthew 21:7).

Prophecy 5: The Messiah will be betrayed by a friend and suffer wounds in His hands (Zechariah 13:6).
Fulfilled: "Judas, one of the twelve, went before them and drew near to Jesus to kiss Him. But Jesus said to him, 'Judas, are you betraying the Son of Man with a kiss?'" (Luke 22:47–48).
Fulfilled: "So he said to them, 'Unless I see in His hands the print of the nails, and put my finger into the print of the nails, and put my hand into His side, I will not believe'" (John 20:25).

Prophecies 6 and 7: The Messiah will be betrayed for thirty pieces of silver and the betrayal money will be used to purchase a potter's field (Zechariah 11:12–13).
Fulfilled: "And they took the thirty pieces of silver, the value of Him who was priced, whom they of the children of Israel priced, and gave them for the potter's field, as the Lord directed me'" (Matthew 27:9–10).

Prophecy 8: The Messiah will remain silent while He is afflicted (Isaiah 53:7).
Fulfilled: "And while He was being accused by the chief priests and elders, He answered nothing. Then Pilate said to Him, 'Do You not hear how many things they testify against You?' But He answered him not one word, so that the governor marveled greatly" (Matthew 27:12–14).

Prophecy 9: Soldiers would gamble for the Messiah's garments (Psalm 22:18).
Fulfilled: "Then Jesus said, 'Father, forgive them, for they do not know what they do.' And they divided His garments and cast lots" (Luke 23:34).

Prophecy 10: The Messiah would be buried with the rich (Isaiah 53:9).
Fulfilled: "Now when evening had come, there came a rich man from Arimathea, named Joseph, who himself had also become a disciple of Jesus. This man went to Pilate and asked for the body of Jesus. Then Pilate commanded the body to be given to him. When Joseph had taken the body, he wrapped it in a clean linen cloth, and laid it in his new tomb which he had hewn out of the rock" (Matthew 27:57–60).

Thoughts and Reflection

Jesus is the Son of God, the Messiah, Savior of the world, and the only way to the Father. Though He lived nearly two thousand years ago, He said, "Heaven and earth will pass away, but My words will by no means pass away" (Matthew 24:35).

Prayer

Dear heavenly Father, thank You for Your Son Jesus, Who died for my sins. Thank You for Your holy scripture. Thank You for Your promises, and for the assurance of eternal life with You.

CLOSING WORDS

The first step in deciding to follow Jesus is answering the same question He posed to His disciples in Matthew 16:15: "Who do you say that I am?" If you believe Jesus Christ is the Son of God and have made a decision to follow Him, you can pray this simple prayer:

"Dear heavenly Father, I know that I am a sinner.[1] Please forgive me.[2] I believe Jesus is Your Son[3] and that You raised Him from the dead.[4] I repent *of* and turn *from* my sinful ways.[5] I humble myself before You, and surrender my life to You.[6] Take control of my life, change me, and make me a new creation.[7] In Jesus' name I pray. Amen."

If you prayed this prayer, set aside time each day to study His word and pray. Find a Bible-believing church and then follow Jesus in believer's baptism.[8] Whether you're a busy parent, grandparent, or a single person with a grinding schedule, God will meet you where you are. No matter what you've done or how unworthy you feel, if you have asked God's forgiveness it is finished. Jesus paid the price for your sins—now, *accept* His forgiveness. Trust Him with your life, the lives of your loved ones, and release your worry, fear, and anxiety to Him.

[1]Romans 3:23: "For all have sinned and fall short of the glory of God."

[2]1 John 1:9: "If we confess our sins, He is faithful and just to forgive us our sins and to cleanse us from all unrighteousness."

[3]Matthew 3:17: "And suddenly a voice *came* from heaven, saying, 'This is My beloved Son, in whom I am well pleased.'"

[4]Matthew 28:5–6: "But the angel answered and said to the women, 'Do not be afraid, for I know that you seek Jesus who was crucified.

He is not here; for He is risen, as He said. Come, see the place where the Lord lay.'"

⁵Acts 3:19: "Repent therefore and be converted, that your sins may be blotted out, so that times of refreshing may come from the presence of the Lord."

⁶James 4:7–8: "Therefore submit to God. Resist the devil and he will flee from you. Draw near to God and He will draw near to you."

⁷2 Corinthians 5:17: "Therefore, if anyone is in Christ, he is a new creation; old things have passed away; behold, all things have become new."

⁸Acts 2:38: "Repent and let every one of you be baptized in the name of Jesus Christ for the remission of sins; and you shall receive the gift of the Holy Spirit."